Lord, I Want To Know You

Lord, I Want to Know You

Kay Arthur

MULTNOMAH BOOKS

Other Books by Kay Arthur:
Lord, Heal My Hurts
Lord, I Need Grace to Make It
Lord, Is it Warfare, Teach Me to Stand
Lord, Where Are You?

Unless otherwise indicated, all Scripture references are from the New American Standard Bible, The Lockman Foundation, ©1960, 1962, 1963, 1968, 1971, 1972, 1973, 1975, 1977. Used by permission.

Scripture references marked KJV are from the Holy Bible: Authorized King James Version.

Permission to quote from the following is gratefully acknowledged:

Jukes, Andres. *The Names of God*. Grand Rapids, Michigan: Kregel Publications, 1976.

Jensen, Irving L. *Jensen's Survey of the Old Testament*. Chicago: Moody Press, 1978. Used by permission.

Bull, Geoffrey T. *God Holds the Key*. Hodder and Stoughton, Ltd., 1960. Reprinted by permission.

Card, Michael and Thompson, John W. "El Shaddai." Whole Armor Publishing Company, 1981.

Cover design by Greg Breeding

LORD, I WANT TO KNOW YOU
© 1992 by Kay Arthur
Published by Multnomah Books
a division of Questar Publishers, Inc.

Printed in the United States of America.

Library of Congress Cataloging-in-Publication Data
Arthur, Kay, 1933-
     Lord,I want to know you: a devotional study on the names of God / Kay Arthur.
         p.   cm.
     ISBN 0-88070-458-6
     1. God—Name—Meditations. I. Title.
BT180.N2A63 1991
231—dc20   91-40978
                                                        CIP

94 95 96 97 98 99 00 01 - 10 9 8 7

CONTENTS

ACKNOWLEDGEMENTS

"For from Him and through Him and to Him are all things" (Romans 11:36). Yet, wonder of wonders, He makes us to be co-laborers together with Him (1 Corinthians 3:9). Any book God would ever use me to write is accomplished because of the concerted efforts of the entire staff of Precept Ministries. Their prayers, love, support, and faithful dedication to the call of God upon their lives in this ministry are God's means of bringing forth this book.

At the head of that team is my dear husband, Jack, the president of Precept Ministries, who encourages me and in numerous ways enables me to persevere in the task God has for me.

I also want to acknowledge two authors who have gone before and have left me and you a legacy of insight into the truths of God's Word and have enabled us to better understand His name and His Word: Dr. Irving Jensen, author of *Jensen's Survey of the Old Testament*, is the one God has used the most to teach me how to study God's Word. His book, *Independent Bible Study*, gave birth to our Precept upon Precept inductive Bible studies. Andrew Jukes, author of *The Names of God*, and Nathan J. Stone, who wrote *Names of God*, are two men to whom I am indebted for

Acknowledgments

insights presented in this book.

And there are all of you . . . who pray for me regularly and encourage me. I have prayed that God would use this book in a transforming way to teach you to know Him in a more intimate way. I know He will answer that prayer according to the measure of your hunger for and your obedience to the truths from His Word contained in this material.

To Him alone, our Jehovah-jireh, our El Shaddai, be the glory forever (Romans 11:36). Amen.

HOW TO
USE THIS BOOK

Do you long to be used of God?

This book can help you fulfill that longing. It can be used as a companion for your individual study or as a guide for group study.

Before you begin, ask God to show you with whom you are to share these truths. Set your own pace, adapting the length of the lessons to the capabilities of your group. At the conclusion of each study of a name of God you will find questions to guide you in group discussion.

As you study, begin practicing the art of hallowing His name.

And one last thing: Would you write me personally and let me know how God has used this book in your life? It will thrill my heart.

Thanks for fulfilling 2 Timothy 2:2.

Love and Maranatha,

O Father, as You
did with Moses,
make all Your goodness
pass before us,
proclaim the name of the
Lord before us,
be gracious unto us and
show us compassion.

A. C. Dixon

THE NAMES OF THE LORD

DAY ONE

The muffled, distant sound had broken the quiet reverie of his walk across the meadow. The sharp barking of a dog almost irritated him. It was abrasive in that tranquil setting. As the barking grew louder his eyes scanned the meadow, looking for the culprit. Suddenly, a small doe broke through the edge of the woods. Now he understood. Leaning against the fence post, the man watched with compassion as the doe cut across the broad expanse of meadow. She was running straight toward him. He stood motionless, not wanting wanting to add the fear of man to the animal's frustration. As the frightened fawn leaped the fence, she staggered.

The Names of the Lord

The chase had taken its toll. Her wet coat gleaming in the sun, the doe stopped, took a few steps in one direction, then, ears held high, looked back toward the sound of the barking. The dog had broken through the woods. Eyes wide with fright, seemingly confused and worn out, the doe surveyed her surroundings until she discovered the man standing beside the fence. Looking back again at the dog in hot pursuit, then at the expanse of open field before her, she turned weakly and walked straight toward the man and buried her head in his tummy. Compassion filled his eyes. She had found a protector.

Where, Beloved, do you run in time of need? When the hounds of trouble, worry, and fear pursue you; when the dogs of temptation, corruption, and evil seek to overtake you; when your energy is spent; when weakness saps you and you feel you cannot run away any longer, where do you turn? *Jesus*

Do you turn to your protector, the One who stands with arms opened wide, waiting for you to come and bury yourself in the security of all He is? *yes*

"The name of the Lord is a strong tower, the righteous runs into it and is safe" (Proverbs 18:10).

For these forty-two days we are going to study the names of the Lord, so that you will know where to run to find help in time of need. The Father longs to have you know Him better, that you might "trust in the name of the LORD and rely" on your God (Isaiah 50:10). This was Jesus' prayer on our behalf just before He went to Calvary, "That they may know Thee, the only true God, and Jesus Christ whom Thou hast sent" (John 17:3). This was the goal of Paul's life, "That I may know Him" (Philippians 3:10). How I pray that it will become the goal of your life!

Let me ask you this: If someone were to ask you to describe God, how would you do it? In the space below, write down the words that come to your mind when you think of God.

All Loving, Patient, Kind, Forgiving

12 *Living, Almighty, merciful, FAIThFull!! Caring, Slow to anger.*

DAY TWO

"Some boast in chariots, and some in horses; but we will boast in the name of the LORD, our God" (Psalm 20:7).

Where do you run for help? When you are in trouble, what is your first instinct? Do you run to others or to God? Is it usually the counsel of another rather than the counsel found in waiting upon God in prayer? Why is this? Why do we run to man before we run to God?

In Old Testament days, chariots and horses were two means of protection and escape. Today our chariots and horses come with different labels, shapes, and forms; even so, they are still a visible means of help, escape, or protection. Yet are these really a source of safety? No. "The horse is prepared against the day of battle: but safety is of the LORD" (Proverbs 21:31, KJV).

What is the problem? Why don't we run to the arms of our all-sufficient God? I think it's because most of us don't really know our God. Why is it that many collapse in the day of trouble and testing? Why is it that they are immobilized rather than taking an aggressive stand in the face of fear? It is because Christians, for the most part, can't boast in the name of their God.

What do I mean when I say, "Boast in the name of our God"? *To boast in* means *to have confidence in, to trust in*. To boast in God's name means to have confidence in His name. In biblical times, a name represented a person's character. God's name represents His character, His attributes, His nature. To know His name is to know Him. To boast in His name is to have confidence in who He is!

In the Bible we find several names of God. You are about to embark on an exciting study of these names. The contents page of this book lists the Old Testament names of God, each with its meaning or definition. These will be our material for study in the days to come.

The Names of the Lord

In the day of trouble or need, we are to run to our God, to put our trust in Him. That is why He says, "Call upon Me in the day of trouble: I will deliver thee, and thou shalt glorify Me" (Psalm 50:15, KJV).

Is your heart troubled? Is fear lurking in the shadows of your consciousness? Do you feel insecure about anything at all? If the answer to any of these questions is yes, list your fears, insecurities, and troubles in the space below. Then pray and ask God to show you one of His names that will meet your need. Then, when He shows you, tell Him that you will boast in that name. *Being cloned, how I look, Talking to people, my weigh*

DAY THREE

Let's begin with a day of meditating on Psalm 20. As you look at this psalm, consider what has been said these past two days. At the end of the psalm you will find a brief assignment. I urge you to participate fully in this study. Don't just read this book. Do the assignments. Write out your answers. This will help cultivate the seeds of truth sown in reading. The harvest can be bountiful, and you will grow!

PSALM 20

May the LORD answer you in the day of trouble! May the name of the God of Jacob set you *securely* on high! May He send you help from the sanctuary, and support you from Zion! May He remember all your meal offerings, and find your burnt offering acceptable! May He grant you your heart's desire, and fulfill all your counsel! We will sing for joy over your victory, and in the name of our God we will set up our banners. May the LORD fulfill all your petitions. Now I know that the LORD saves His anointed; He will answer him from His holy heaven, with the saving strength of His right hand. Some *boast* in chariots, and some in horses; but we

will boast in the name of the LORD, our God.
They have bowed down and fallen; but we
have risen and stood upright. Save, O LORD;
may the King answer us in the day we call.

1. Go through this psalm and put a ⬤ around
every word that has something to do with trouble,
need, or help.

2. What are the Lord's promises in this psalm?

*He will grant me my hearts
desire, and fulfill all my
needs.*

3. Are there any conditions that need to be met in
order for the promises to be fulfilled?

*I need to boast in His name
& rise & stand upright for the
Lord*

4. According to this psalm, what sets a person
securely on high or in security above the circumstances of a situation? *The name of the
God of Jacob.*

5. On what basis can we set up banners of victory?

*In the name of our
God.*

6. What does the answer to question 5 tell you about the name of God?

That in the name of God we can conquer anything.

7. Why are they boasting in the name of the Lord?

To show our love for Him. To have confidence & trust in Him

DISCUSSION QUESTIONS FOR DAYS 1 THROUGH 3

1. Before the study of these first three days, how did you picture God in your mind? *Loving, forgiving, Faithful.*

2. What was so significant about a name in biblical times? *A name represented a person character.*

3. Why is it important that we know the name of our God? *To know His name, is to know Him.*

4. In Psalm 20, God talks about men who boast in chariots and horses and men who boast in the name of the Lord. Did you see a contrast between these two types of people? What is the contrast? *One is boasting in self & one is boasting in God.*

5. What does trusting in horses and chariots mean? How does that apply to today? *Trusting in the Flesh, Instead of relying on the Lord, People tend to rely on Self.*

6. Can you remember a time when you trusted in "horses and chariots"? What was the result in your life? *I fell, and nothing worked in my life.*

7. Can you remember a time when you boasted in the name of the Lord? What was the result?

I boast in the name of the Lord, and the results are unexplainable, He is always faithful, and He fulfills all my desires & needs.

THE CREATOR

DAY FOUR

One of the names of God in the Old Testament is *Elohim*. It designates God as God. Deuteronomy 10:17 says, "The LORD your God [Elohim] is the God of gods . . ." *El* means mighty or strong and is used for any reference to gods, including Almighty God. Elohim is the primary word translated God in the Old Testament. (Sometimes *Jehovah* is translated God rather than Lord.) The *him* ending of Elohim is very significant, for it is a plural ending in the Hebrew that indicates three or more. Elohim, the name for God as Creator, is used in Genesis 1:1 and could be translated,

"In the beginning Gods created the heavens and the earth."

Does this mean there is more than one God? No! "The LORD [Jehovah] is our God [Elohim], the LORD is one" (Deuteronomy 6:4). God the Father, God the Son, and God the Holy Spirit—the blessed Trinity—created the heavens and the earth. One in essence, in character, yet three persons united as one. As you read various scriptures, you can see references to the different persons of the Godhead participating in the work of creation. In Genesis 1:2-3 we read, "The Spirit of God was moving over the surface of the waters. Then God said, 'Let there be light'; and there was light." "By faith we understand that the worlds were prepared by the word of God . . ." (Hebrews 11:3). God spoke, the Spirit moved, and Colossians 1:16 tells us that in Him, in Jesus Christ, the Son of God, "all things were created, both in the heavens and on earth." Thus, we see that each person of the triune Godhead had a part in creation. This is seen even in the creation of man, for in Genesis 1:26 we read, "Then God [Elohim] said, 'Let Us make man in Our image.'" The *Us* has to refer to more than one!

But of what practical significance is this name to us? How can the name Elohim serve as a strong tower to us?

If God is the Creator of all things, if "all things have been created through Him and for Him" (Colossians 1:16), who has given us life? Elohim, of course! And why were we created? For Him! You are a unique creation of God, one of a kind, created for His glory. He "didst form my inward parts." He "didst weave me in my mother's womb. . . . I am fearfully and wonderfully made" (Psalm 139:13-14). Have you ever thought of yourself as being fearfully and wonderfully made? Or do you look at yourself and despise what Elohim has created?

I have a friend who is probably not more than three feet tall. Her head is of normal size, and to me she is lovely. Yet, Julie spends all her days in a sling, much like a baby's walker. In order for her to move anywhere, her legs must push the rolling frame. Julie is radiant, a delight to all who meet her, but then she knows her Elohim, and she realizes that He created her this way for a purpose. Now, please don't tell me God had nothing to do with her physical condition. If so, I must deny His sovereignty, His Word, and His name.

Remember when "Moses said to the LORD, 'Please, Lord, I have never been eloquent, neither recently nor in time past, nor since Thou hast spoken to Thy servant; for I am slow of speech and slow of tongue'" (Exodus 4:10).

And what was the Lord's reply? "Who has made man's mouth? Or who makes him dumb or deaf, or seeing or blind? Is it not I, the LORD?" (Exodus 4:11).

But why would God create people who are different from His normal pattern of creation? Why would He ever permit a sperm to penetrate an egg when it would produce what seems to be a genetic disaster?

Remember when the disciples saw a man blind from birth, "and His disciples asked Him, saying, 'Rabbi, who sinned, this man or his parents, that he should be born blind?'" (John 9:2)? How did Jesus answer? "It was neither that this man sinned, nor his parents; but it was in order that the works of God might be displayed in him" (John 9:3).

Oh, Beloved, if you are not happy with yourself, with your child, or with a loved one, run into the strong tower of the name of your Elohim (Proverbs 18:10). You may not understand how your situation could ever bring Him glory, but you can trust in the name of your Lord. "Who is among you that fears the LORD, that obeys the voice of His servant, that walks in darkness and has no light? Let him trust in the name of the LORD and rely on his God" (Isaiah 50:10).

"I will give thanks to the LORD according to His righteousness, and will sing praise to the name of the LORD Most High" (Psalm 7:17). "For the LORD [Jehovah] your God [Elohim] is the God [Elohim] of gods [Elohim] and the Lord [Jehovah] of lords, the great, the mighty, and the awesome God . . ." (Deuteronomy 10:17). Write out a prayer of worship to your creator. Sing praise to your God and Father as Elohim.

> Oh, Elohim you are my mighty savior, the Stronghold In my life, Please Elohim give me The knowledge to know you better! I love you my Jehovah!!

"For from Him and through Him and to Him are all things. To Him be the glory forever. Amen" (Romans 11:36).

DAY FIVE

You have heard the song. The words go, "Why was I born? Why am I living?" They are more than words to a song, aren't they? They are the heart's cry of every human being who seeks to know the reason for his existence.

Why were you born? Why did Elohim create you? Why did He form your inward parts and weave you in your mother's womb (Psalm 139:13)? Search out the answer to these questions, and you will know the purpose for your life.

In the forty-third chapter of Isaiah, we read, "Thus says the LORD, your Creator, O Jacob, and He who formed you, O Israel. . . . I am the LORD your God [Elohim] . . . you are precious in My sight . . . every one who is called by My name, and whom I have created for My glory, whom I have formed, even whom I have made" (Isaiah 43:1,3-4,7).

According to Isaiah 43, Elohim, the one who made man (male and female, Genesis 1:27) in His image, created you for His glory.

One day while studying what God's Word says about the husband-wife relationship, I decided that since "woman is the glory of man" (1 Corinthians 11:7) I had better look up the meaning of the word *glory*. It means to give the correct opinion or estimate of. I saw that as a woman I am to treat my husband in such a way as to give a correct opinion or estimate of him as a man.

Can you see how awesome it is to know that you have been created for God's glory? That you are to live in such a way as to give all of creation a correct opinion or estimate of who God is? What does that mean to you, O child of God, who is called by His name? Think about it. How would you live if you were to live for His glory? Give yourself time to meditate on this truth, and then record below those things that God brings to your mind.

I would live completely for God, give up everything to him. I would tell everyone about him & how awesomely great he is. I will treat my body as his temple for which it is.

Let me show you one other scripture that tells you why you were born. "Worthy art Thou, our Lord and our God, to receive glory and honor and power; for Thou didst create all things, and because of Thy will they existed, and were created" (Revelation 4:11). According to this scripture, you were created for His will. The King James Version says "pleasure." In essence, they are the same. If I live for His will, that is,

The Creator

His pleasure, or if I bring Him pleasure, it is because I have done His will.

His name is Elohim, the Almighty God, your Creator. You have looked at two scriptures that have answered the questions, "Why was I born? Why am I living?" You have seen that you have been created for His glory, for His pleasure. Your life is to be lived in such a way as to reflect Him, to show the world the character of God, His love, His peace, His mercy, His gentleness. You are to live for Him, to accomplish His will. To miss this is to miss fulfillment. It is to have existed rather than to have lived.

Go before your God and evaluate the course of your life. Are you fulfilling the purpose of your creation? What is keeping you from being or doing what you were created for? What do you need to change? What do you need to do? Will you? Answer these questions honestly in the presence of your Elohim. Then, when you finish, write out a prayer of commitment.

Dear my Elohim, help me to fulfil your purpose for me Lord help me to be able to minister to everyone who need to know your name. For you are my creator, and I want to live solely for you Lord. Give me the wisdom my Elohim to know how & what to say to people in need of you. I will glorify you Lord for I love you! Amen.

24

DISCUSSION QUESTIONS FOR DAYS 4 AND 5

1. Elohim identifies God as Creator. From your study, why do you think it is important to know Him as Creator? *Because it gives you reasons why you are here, & what He wants of you.*

2. What did God create? *For His Glory, God created everything*

3. How does Elohim as Creator show us the triune God? *God spoke, the spirit moved & in to the name of Jesus Christ all things were created*

4. What role has God had in your life? *God is my life.*

5. What is your responsibility to Him as your Creator? How are you fulfilling that responsibility? *to Glorify him. I live only for Him.*

6. How have the insights into God as Elohim helped to clear up your thinking regarding children born with Down's syndrome or those born without a limb? *God made the so that his works can be shown through them.*

7. What is happening in your life or circumstances right now that is easier to deal with now that you know your God, your Elohim?

I think knowing God as my Elohim helps me through each day of serving him easier. For I want to be God's complete Glory.

It has helped me to understand why I'm here, and why God has made me the way I am.

THE GOD MOST HIGH

DAY SIX

Not only is God our Elohim, He is also our *El Elyon*, the Most High. El Elyon is the name that designates God as the sovereign ruler of all the universe. It was El Elyon, "God Most High, who has delivered" Abraham's enemies into his hand (Genesis 14:20). It was the Most High God who was and is the Redeemer of Israel (Psalm 78:35). And it is the Most High God who rules today over the affairs of men. "For His dominion is an everlasting dominion, and His kingdom endures from generation to generation. And all the inhabitants of the earth are accounted as nothing, but He does according to His will in the host of heaven and among the inhabitants of earth; and no one can ward off His hand or say to Him, 'What hast Thou done?'" (Daniel 4:34-35). Thus "Nebuchadnezzar . . . blessed the Most High and praised and honored Him who lives forever" (Daniel 4:34).

If "the name of the God of Jacob" would "set you securely on high," if you would trust Him to "send you help from the sanctuary, and support you from Zion" (Psalm 20:1-2), then you must know Him as El Elyon, the Most High. For if God is not sovereign, if He is not in control, if all things are not under His dominion, then He is not the Most High, and you and I are either in the hands of fate (whatever that is), in the hands of man, or in the hands of the devil.

Below are some scriptures that show the sovereignty of El Elyon. Read each passage carefully. Then, in the space that follows, write an analysis of how that particular passage shows God's sovereignty or over what He has supremacy. Think about each one carefully.

Daniel 4:34-35

But at the end of that period I, Nebuchadnezzar, raised my eyes toward heaven, and my reason returned to me, and I blessed the Most High and praised and honored Him who lives forever; for His dominion is an everlasting dominion, and His kingdom endures from generation to generation. And all the inhabitants of the earth are accounted as nothing, but He does according to His will in the host of heaven and among the inhabitants of earth; and no one can ward off His hand or say to Him, "What hast Thou done?"

He is the ruler over all the heavens & earth & we shall praise & honor him.

ISAIAH 14:24,27

The LORD of hosts has sworn saying, "Surely, just as I have intended so it has happened, and just as I have planned so it will stand. . . . For the LORD of hosts has planned, and who can frustrate it? And as for His stretched-out hand, who can turn it back?"

Everything he has planned + intended will happen & no one can change that.

ISAIAH 46:9-11

Remember the former things long past, for I am God, and there is no other; I *am* God, and there is no one like Me, declaring the end from the beginning and from ancient times things which have not been done, saying, "My purpose will be established, and I will accomplish all My good pleasure"; calling a bird of prey from the east, the man of My purpose from a far country. Truly I have spoken; truly I will bring it to pass. I have planned it, *surely* I will do it.

He is the one + only God. + he declared the beginning + end, + he will accomplish all this good pleasure as he has planned it

DANIEL 2:20-23

Daniel answered and said, "Let the name of God be blessed forever and ever, for wisdom and power belong to Him. And it is He who changes the times and the epochs; He removes kings and establishes kings; He gives wisdom to wise men, and knowledge to men of understanding. It is He who reveals the profound and hidden things; He knows what is in the darkness, and the light dwells with Him. To Thee, O God of my fathers, I give thanks and

Wisdom + Power belong to him. He gives man all they have. + he gives to all the light that dwells in him.

29

praise, for Thou hast given me wisdom and power; even now Thou hast made known to me what we requested of Thee, for Thou hast made known to us the king's matter."

He is the ruler over all matters.

We will continue tomorrow. But first let's take what you have learned today and see how it can apply to your life. What difference does it make in your life when you realize God is sovereign, that He is Ruler over all, and that nothing can happen without the ultimate sanction or permission of God?

It makes me want to understand him even more, & get as close as I can to him.

DAY SEVEN

Today I want us to continue to look at scriptures that specifically deal with various aspects of El Elyon's sovereignty. Remember, follow each passage with your written analysis of how that passage shows God's sovereignty, or with a statement showing that over which He rules.

ISAIAH 5:5-7

"So now let Me tell you what I am going to do to My vineyard: I will remove its hedge and it will be consumed; I will break down its wall and it will become trampled ground. And I will lay it waste; it will not be pruned or hoed, but briars and thorns will come up. I will also charge the clouds to rain no rain on it." For the vineyard of the LORD of hosts is the house of

Israel, and the men of Judah His delightful plant. Thus He looked for justice, but behold, bloodshed; for righteousness, but behold, a cry of distress.

Note who the vineyard is. *we all are his vineyard. He rule over all us & our land.*

DEUTERONOMY 32:39

See now that I, I am He, and there is no god besides Me; it is I who put to death and give life. I have wounded, and it is I who heal; and there is no one who can deliver from My hand.

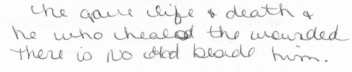

he gave life & death & he who heal the wounded there is no God beside him.

1 SAMUEL 1:5-6

But to Hannah he would give a double portion, for he loved Hannah, but the LORD had closed her womb. Her rival, however, would provoke her bitterly to irritate her, because the LORD had closed her womb.

1 SAMUEL 2:6-10

The LORD kills and makes alive; He brings down to Sheol and raises up. The LORD makes poor and rich; He brings low, He also exalts. He raises the poor from the dust, He lifts the needy from the ash heap to make them sit with nobles, and inherit a seat of honor; for the pillars of the earth are the LORD's, and He set the world on them. He keeps the feet of His godly ones, but the wicked ones are silenced in darkness; for not by might shall a man prevail. Those who contend with the LORD will be shattered; against them He will thunder in the heavens, the LORD will judge the ends of the earth; and He will give strength to His king, and will exalt the horn of His anointed.

ISAIAH 45:6-7

I am the LORD, and there is no other, the One forming light and creating darkness, causing well-being and creating calamity; I am the LORD who does all these.

JOHN 19:10-11

Pilate therefore said to Him, "You do not speak to me? Do You not know that I have authority to release You, and I have authority to crucify You?" Jesus answered, "You would have no authority over Me, unless it had been given you from above; for this reason he who delivered Me up to you has the greater sin."

Now consider the next passage.

JOB 2:1-10

Again there was a day when the sons of God came to present themselves before the LORD, and Satan also came among them to present himself before the LORD. And the LORD said to Satan, "Where have you come from?" Then Satan answered the LORD and said, "From roaming about on the earth, and walking around on it." And the LORD said to Satan, "Have you considered My servant Job? For there is no one like him on the earth, a blameless and upright man fearing God and turning away from evil. And he still holds fast his integrity, although you incited Me against him, to ruin him without cause." And Satan answered the LORD and said, "Skin for skin! Yes, all that a man has he will give for his life. However, put forth Thy hand, now, and touch his bone and his flesh; he will curse Thee to Thy face." So the LORD said to Satan, "Behold, he is in your power, only spare his life." Then Satan went out from the presence of the LORD, and smote Job with sore boils from the sole of his foot to the crown of his head. And he took a potsherd to scrape himself while he was sitting among the ashes. Then his wife said to him, "Do you still hold fast your integrity? Curse God and die!" But he said to her, "You speak as one of the foolish women speaks. Shall we indeed accept good from God and not accept adversity?" In all this Job did not sin with his lips.

1. What did God point out to Satan about Job?

2. What reason does Satan give for Job's response to his trials of chapter 1?

3. What did Satan propose for Job? Why?

4. What was God's response?

5. Who was in control?

Now one last verse. In it, Simon is the apostle Peter.

Luke 22:31

Simon, Simon, behold, Satan has demanded [or obtained by asking] permission to sift you like wheat.

1. How does Luke 22:31 show Satan's relationship to God?

2. Finally, in several sentences summarize what you learned today.

DAY NINE

The truth of God's sovereignty makes it easier to obey those commands in the New Testament that charge us to rejoice in all circumstances of life. God tells us that we are to "be filled with the Spirit . . . always giving thanks for all things in the name of our Lord Jesus Christ to God, even the Father" (Ephesians 5:18,20).

Doesn't this become easier when you know that your Father, El Elyon, God Most High, is in control and that nothing can happen in His universe without His permission? Even when we are wronged by others, we can still give thanks. Although we have been given a free will, still God so rules and overrules that no person, angel, demon, or devil, nor any circumstance of life, can thwart His plan.

El Elyon rules supremely over all. And because He does, you can understand how all things "work together for good to those who love God, to those who are called according to His purpose" (Romans 8:28). In everything you can "give thanks; for this is God's will for you in Christ Jesus" (1 Thessalonians 5:18).

Do you remember how Joseph's brothers plotted his demise? Because of his brothers' jealousy, Joseph was sold to be a slave in Egypt. There, in the house of Potiphar, he was falsely accused and put in prison for two years. It was enough to make any normal man bitter at God. Joseph had done what was right, had been faithful to his God, and suffered because of it. He seemed the victim of the whims and plots of men. And yet, not once during all this time did Joseph do anything but honor his God (Genesis 39:9; 40:8; 41:25,28).

He knew the Most High stood in the shadows ruling over all, watching and waiting. Whether or not he understood, Joseph knew that God had a purpose in it all. How can I say that? Because of what Joseph said to his brothers when they found themselves standing before him as the appointed ruler over all Egypt (Genesis 42:6). "And now do not be grieved or angry with yourselves, because you sold me here; for God sent me before you to preserve life. . . . And God sent me before you to preserve for you a remnant in the earth, and to keep you alive by a great deliverance. Now, therefore, it was not you who sent me here, but God; and He has made me a father to Pharaoh and lord of all his household and ruler over all the land of Egypt. . . And as for you, you meant evil against me, but God meant it for good in order to bring about this present result, to preserve many people alive" (Genesis 45:5,7-8; 50:20).

O Beloved, the next time you start to murmur or complain, run to your El Elyon, trust in His name, and give thanks.

1. How would you explain the meaning of El Elyon to another person?

2. How would you explain the sovereignty of God?

3. El Elyon is the Most High God. If you could really understand what that means, what would it alter in your thinking about:
   a. your government
   b. your financial circumstances
   c. your marriage
   d. your children
   e. your parents
   f. Satan

4. How does the study of the name of El Elyon help you better understand the instruction, "in everything give thanks; for this is God's will for you in Christ Jesus" (1 Thessalonians 5:18)?

5. From the study on El Elyon, how limited is Satan? Who sets his limits?

6. If God is sovereign, why does He let Satan have his way in certain circumstances? Think carefully through your study on Job.

7. How did the sovereignty of God manifest itself in the life of Joseph?

8. How do you see El Elyon's work in your own life?

THE GOD WHO SEES

DAY TEN

Thrown out! Like a soiled, worthless rag! Used for another's pleasure and then mistreated. It was too much; she couldn't handle it. She felt like an outcast. That was Hagar, the one who bore the son of Sarai's husband, Abram.

Have you ever been thrown out, cast away? You fulfilled someone's pleasure and then you weren't wanted anymore? Did you run away? Or were you unjustly cast out?

Do you wonder if there was some way in which

you failed or were inadequate? Maybe if you had behaved differently, maybe if you had been more than you were, maybe if only you . . . the speculations go on.

People tell you that it wasn't your fault; you weren't the only one who was wrong. But right or wrong, you will feel rejection deep inside and with rejection comes that feeling of inadequacy.

Where is God? you ask. Where is this sovereign God who promises that all things work together for good? Does He know what is going on? Does He see?

Yes, He is El Roi, the God who sees. The omnipresent God is there and His eyes are not shut. He isn't asleep, unaware of all the circumstances. He sees.

Stop and read Genesis 16, then answer the following questions.

1. List all that you learn about Hagar from this chapter.

2. Whose idea was it that Abram and Hagar have relations? Why?

3. Do you think Hagar had much of a choice in this decision? What makes you answer the way you do?

4. What provoked Sarai and how did she respond?

5. Was Hagar totally innocent in all this?

6. Do you in any way relate to Hagar or her situation? How?

7. What were God's instructions to Hagar?

8. What did Hagar learn about God?

9. Knowing what you do about God, how would it help to also know Him as El Roi? Make sure you answer the why of it also; it is so important.

DAY ELEVEN

So God sees!

Many times when we are mistreated, used by someone we trusted or respected, we tend to bury the situation. The memory of it, the emotions, the rejection all seem too much to bear so we "stuff it." I guess we think that if we stuff it, it will go away.

But our computer-like memory bank stores it, but then something happens and the program is called up and replayed on the screen of our memory. The pain, the bitterness, the recriminations are too much—so once again, it's stuffed.

Some time ago I did five television programs on incest. The mail came in. I wept; I hurt; I was horrified. How could people do these things to others? Many told their story for the first time. Years had passed, yet for most there had been no healing. They had stuffed it. Some even wondered if they were dreaming. How could anything so unnatural, so horrible be real? But . . . they knew they weren't dreaming.

How could they ever be whole? How can any

abused person, any person used for another's perverted pleasure, ever be whole? Whether it be sexual, mental, or physical abuse, can there be healing? Yes, healing has to be possible. Otherwise, a sovereign God of love would surely have intervened.

Where does healing begin? Healing begins with the recognition of El Roi, the God who sees. He was awake. He saw it all.

The first time we meet God in the Word as El Roi we find Him telling Hagar to go back and deal with the situation. If you have been a victim of incest you need to get it out, face it, and deal with what happened as it really was. God saw it all—there is no hiding the facts from Him. "Where can I go from Thy Spirit? Or where can I flee from Thy presence? If I ascend to heaven, Thou art there; if I make my bed in Sheol, behold, Thou art there. If I take the wings of the dawn, if I dwell in the remotest part of the sea, even there Thy hand will lead me, and Thy right hand will lay hold of me. If I say, 'Surely the darkness will overwhelm me, and the light around me will be night,' even the darkness is not dark to Thee, and the night is as bright as the day. Darkness and light are alike to Thee" (Psalm 139:7-12).

God saw it. He knows the sin that was committed against you. And someday He will vindicate you. There is forgiveness, but to those who refuse to receive the Lamb of God who takes away the sins of the world, there is also a day of judgment. And it will be a righteous judgment, for God saw it all (2 Thessalonians 1:5-10).

After you realize that He sees, you need to know that in His sovereignty He permitted it. Therefore, as horrible and as destructive as it seems, in God's economy it will be used for good if you will but know Him, believe Him, and put your trust in His name, for He does not forsake those who seek Him (Psalm 9:10).

That is one way it helps to know His name El Roi. The second is this: If you have loved ones out there who have run away, although you do not know where they are or what is happening in their lives, El Roi does. He sees. You can't, but He can. Run into the strong tower of His name and rest. You will learn more about your God through His names. These truths will be your comfort, your healing, your sanity, your hope, your protection against the fiery darts of the accusing liar. Today, stop and think of any other ways it would help to know God as El Roi. List these below.

Discussion Questions for Days 10 and 11

1. What were the circumstances surrounding the revelation of God as El Roi?

2. How did you feel about what was done to Hagar? Does it parallel anything that ever happened in your own life?

3. Would it have helped you at all to know God as El Roi? How?

4. What do you think about dealing with cases of abuse in the way the author describes?

5. In what other situations would it help to know God as El Roi? How? Be specific and practical.

THE ALL-SUFFICIENT ONE

DAY TWELVE

Until I was twenty-nine, I longed to be held in the arms of a man. I wanted security, and I thought that it was to be found in a man who would draw me to himself, lay my head on his chest and become my protector, my sustainer for life. To me this was the epitome of life. It was all I wanted.

I didn't find it in my first husband. On the second day of our honeymoon, my husband—my capable, talented, athletic husband—went into depression. Instead of being loving and protecting, Tom began to tell me all the things he didn't like about me and that he wanted changed. That was just the beginning of the ups and downs of his mood swings. Some days were wonderful. On those days I loved keeping his house, entertaining his friends, and being his wife. But when he would become depressed, my protector was gone and I would fight for survival. I was determined not to be destroyed.

We went to church. We knew the name *God.* We knew His Son's name, Jesus. We bore His name, Christian. But we really didn't know Him. We thought we did. We never heard or saw anything that would make us question whether we were Christians. But then if we knew any real Christians, I was not aware of it. We were all the same. We all played church.

Finally, I couldn't handle the depression anymore. I was too self-centered. I left Tom and took our sons Tommy and Mark with me. Yet the longing for security remained. I wanted to be held. I wanted to be loved just as I was, no strings attached—loved whether I was pretty or ugly, sick or well, in a good mood or a bad mood. I wanted to be loved regardless of what I was like. I wanted to be loved unconditionally.

I began my search. I went from one man to another. In the process, I became something I never wanted, never dreamed I would ever be. I became an adulteress. Yet all I wanted was security.

When I was twenty-nine, my search ended on my knees beside my bed, for there I met my El Shaddai. Have you heard that song on the names of God? "El Shaddai, El Shaddai, El Elyonna, Adonai; I will praise you 'til I die, El Shaddai."

Whenever you see God almighty in the Old Testament, you see your El Shaddai.

When Abraham first knew God as His El Shaddai, he fell on his face (Genesis 17:1-3). Time and time again I have found Him to be my all-sufficient God, my protector, the unconditional lover of my soul. He held me through the suicide of my first husband. He held me as a single parent when at times I was overwhelmed by loneliness, responsibility, and the need to be held. He has held me through times of great financial need, both personally and in our ministry. He has held me when the pains of leadership have seemed almost overwhelming. He has held me when I have failed. He has held me when I have cried for my children and poured out my doubts about being a good mother. He has held me when I have been afraid because of what He has told me to speak to others. He has held me when I have had no more strength and have wondered how I would ever make it. He has held me when I felt overwhelmed by all that I had to do. When I have run to Him, I have never come away wanting. He is my El Shaddai, my all-sufficient One. O Beloved, do you understand? Have you experienced Him as your El Shaddai? If not, He is waiting, arms open wide for you.

Let's look at the time when God first revealed Himself as El Shaddai:

GENESIS 17:1-8

Now when Abram was ninety-nine years old, the LORD appeared to Abram and said to him, "I am God Almighty; walk before Me, and be blameless. And I will establish My covenant between Me and you, and I will multiply you exceedingly." And Abram fell on his face, and God talked with him, saying, "As for Me, behold, My covenant is with you, and you shall be the father of a multitude of nations. No longer shall your name be called Abram, but your name shall be Abraham; for I will make you the father of a multitude of nations. And I will make you exceedingly fruitful, and I will make nations of you, and kings shall come forth from you. And I will establish My covenant between Me and you and your descendants after you throughout their generations for an everlasting covenant, to be God to you and to your descendants after you. And I will give to you and to your descendants after you, the land of your sojournings, all the land of Canaan, for an everlasting possession; and I will be their God."

If anyone needed to know God as El Shaddai, it was Abraham. He was ninety-nine years old and Sarah was eighty-nine, and still they were childless. Yet, God had promised them a child of their own. "And without becoming weak in faith he contemplated his own body, now as good as dead since he was about a hundred years old, and the deadness of Sarah's womb" (Romans 4:19). How could Abraham give glory to God in such a seemingly hopeless situation? It was because he knew Him as El Shaddai.

El (and its derivatives Elim, Elohim, Eloah) is "one of the oldest and most widely distributed terms for Deity known to the human race."[1] Remember, El actually stands for might or power; and when it is not used for God, it is still translated might or power (Genesis 31:29). The translation of *Shaddai* is not as clear in its meaning, for scholars are not absolutely sure of its root word. Some feel that it speaks of God in His might and power as seen in His judgments. Others lean toward the definition I have given you, the all-sufficient One.

The following quote from *The Names of God* by Andrew Jukes is a lengthy one, but well worth consideration:

The thought expressed in the name "Shaddai" . . . describes power, but it is the power, not of violence, but of all-bountifulness. "Shaddai" primarily means "Breasted," being formed directly from the Hebrew word Shad, that is, "the breast," or, more exactly, a "woman's breast." Parkhurst thus explains the name— "Shaddai, one of the Divine titles, meaning *The Pourer or Shedder forth,* that is, of blessings, temporal and spiritual. . . ."

If this is seen, I need hardly explain how this title, the "Breasted," or the "Pourer-forth," came to mean "Almighty." Mothers at least will understand it. A babe is crying—restless. Nothing can quiet it. Yes: the breast can. A babe is pining—starving. Its life is going out. It cannot take man's proper food: it will die. No: the breast can give it fresh life, and nourish it. By her breast the mother has almost infinite power over the child. . . .

This is "El Shaddai," the "Pourer-forth," who pours Himself out for His creatures; who gives them His lifeblood; who "sheds forth His Spirit," and says, "Come unto me and drink:" "Open thy mouth wide and I will fill it:" and who thus, by the sacrifice of Himself, gives Himself and His very nature to those who will receive Him, that thus His perfect will may be accomplished in them. The blessed Sacrament of the body and blood of Christ is the ceaseless witness of this giving Himself to us. We may, and we must, "Eat His flesh and drink His blood," if He is to live and work His works in us. Only so, "if we eat His flesh and drink His blood," can we "abide in Him and He in us." Only so, in virtue of His indwelling, can He fulfill His purpose, and be Almighty in us. And yet this giving of Himself involves judgment: self-judgment, if we are obedient: if disobedient, the judgment of the Lord.

This is the truth which the name, "El Shaddai," or "Almighty," everywhere proclaims. But it nowhere comes out more clearly than in the record of the LORD's dealings with Abram, when this name, "Almighty," was first revealed to him. Abram had long been the heir of promise. As yet he knew not "Jehovah," but the Lord had promised to bless him, and to give him an inheritance, and a seed which should be as the dust of the earth for multitude. But Abram was yet childless. Moved, however, by the promise of God, in his own energy, and by a bond-maid, he makes efforts to obtain that which was to come to him, not in his own strength, but by God's Almightiness. Then comes the revelation of "El Shaddai." God gives Himself to Abram, and then Abram perfectly gives himself to God, and by God is made fruitful. First, the LORD says, "I am God Almighty." Here is the revelation of the source from which Abram is to receive everything. Then He adds something to Abram's name. He puts something into Abram, which at once changes him from Abram to Abraham. What He adds is the letter He, (ה), the chief letter of His own name "Jehovah,"—that sound which can only be uttered by an outbreathing—thus giving to the elect something of His own nature, (for name denotes nature,) and so by the communication of Himself and of His outbreath or spirit, molding His creature to His own pleasure, that he may be a channel of blessing to many others. At once Abram yields himself to "God Almighty" in everything:—first, in the outward act of circumcision, that figure of self-judgment and perfect self-surrender, which testified that his hope was not in the flesh, or its energies, but only in the blessed Giver of Himself, by whom alone we can bring forth the fruit that is accepted of Him: and then no less in the giving up and sacrifice of the much-loved son, who had so long been waited for, and of whom it had been said, "In Isaac shall thy seed be called;" that thus, in the utter renunciation of himself and of his own will, the power of "Almighty God" might be brought in, and the elect in his weakness be made strong, and in his giving up of all be filled with all the fullness of his God.

This was the lesson Abram learned from the revelation of the name, "El Shaddai." This is the lesson we must all learn, if we too are to know God as "Almighty," able to fulfill his purpose in us, and from fruitless Abrams to make us Abrahams, that is the "fathers of a multitude."

Seeing God as your El Shaddai, can you appreciate Paul's words even more: "And He has said to me, 'My grace is sufficient for you, for power is perfected in weakness.' Most gladly, therefore, I will rather boast about my weaknesses, that the power of Christ may dwell in me. Therefore I am well content with weaknesses, with insults, with distresses, with persecutions, with difficulties, for Christ's sake; for when I am weak, then I am strong" (2 Corinthians 12:9-10).

As God spoke to Abraham thousands of years ago, so He speaks the same words to you, "I am God Almighty [El Shaddai]; walk before Me, and be blameless" (Genesis 17:1).

DISCUSSION QUESTIONS FOR DAY 12

1. Some think that El Shaddai means the all-sufficient One. Why?

2. What did this revelation of God mean to Abram? How did he respond to that revelation?

3. How does 2 Corinthians 12:9-10 apply to God's name, El Shaddai?

4. What are some of the things you have looked to for satisfaction? Did these satisfy?

5. Has God revealed Himself to you as El Shaddai? What has that meant in your life?

El Shaddai
all-sufficient one

THE
LORD

Day Thirteen

Before you can ever really know God as El Shaddai, the all-sufficient One, I believe you must bow before Him as Adonai, your Lord and Master. On the day I was saved I could never have known the refuge of His arms without first bowing my knee and acknowledging His right to rule over me. When I came to Him on July 16, 1963, I said, "Lord, You can do anything You want with me." On that day of days, I did not know that Adonai was one of His names, but I had come to the place of total commitment to the will of God. And when I acknowledged

Him as my Lord, I found my El Shaddai.

Do you realize how many people are disappointed with their Christianity? It just does not seem to satisfy, so they give themselves to temporal things. Is it that Christianity does not satisfy or that they have never experienced true Christianity? Look at those who claim to be children of God. How many individuals do you see whose earnest expectation and hope is, "that I shall not be put to shame in anything, but that with all boldness, Christ shall even now, as always, be exalted in my body, whether by life or by death" (Philippians 1:20)? How many do you know who live a life that says, "For to me, to live is Christ, and to die is gain" (Philippians 1:21)? Why are there so few? Now don't write off these types as the fanatics, the super saints, the ones whose duty it is to live that life because they are called to full-time service of some sort. Commitment to the will of God ought to be the norm for every one of His children.

"But," you may ask, "if that's the norm, where does that leave most of the people in the church?" Study His name, Adonai, and the scriptures that relate to Him as Lord, and then see how you would answer that question. For a start, read what Jesus said in His Sermon on the Mount: "And why do you call Me, 'Lord, Lord,' and do not do what I say?" (Luke 6:46). "Not everyone who says to Me, 'Lord, Lord,' will enter the kingdom of heaven; but he who does the will of My Father who is in heaven. Many will say to Me on that day, 'Lord, Lord, did we not prophesy in Your name, and in Your name cast out demons, and in Your name perform many miracles?" And then I will declare to them, 'I never knew you; DEPART FROM ME, YOU WHO PRACTICE LAWLESSNESS'" (Matthew 7:21-23).

But does it matter what I do as long as I acknowledge Him as Lord and tell Him I want His free gift of eternal life? Yes, it does, for *Lord* is more than a word; it indicates a relationship. The lordship of God means

His total possession of me and my total submission to Him as Lord and Master. Look at how this name of God, Adonai, is used in Scripture. Then you can decide whether or not you can honestly say, "Lord, Lord." That is the bottom line, isn't it?

Adonai, Lord, is first used in Genesis 15:2.

Remember now, El Shaddai was not used until Genesis 17. We studied the meaning of El Shaddai before Adonai because it is easier to call Him El Shaddai than it is to call Him Adonai. Yet, you will never know His sufficiency apart from knowing Him as Lord, as Master. Only a servant can be totally dependent upon his master to meet all his needs. I am sure Abraham understood this, for slavery was common in his day.

Abraham, having won a great victory, gave a tenth of all he possessed to that illustrious, mysterious, and somewhat elusive king of Salem, Melchizedek. At this time, Melchizedek, the priest of God Most High (El Elyon), said: "Blessed by Abram of God Most High, Possessor of heaven and earth; and blessed be God Most High, Who has delivered your enemies into your hand" (Genesis 14:19-20).

Having known victory over his enemies and having understood that El Elyon, the sovereign God, brought about the victory, Abraham acknowledges God's lordship over him. This is the first such recorded instance in the Bible. In Genesis 14:22 Abraham referred to God as Lord (Jehovah), God Most High (El Elyon). But not until Genesis 15:2 does Abraham address God as his master when he says, "O Lord [Adonai] GOD [Jehovah]." The literal Hebrew rendering of God in this verse in YHWH, Jehovah, and thus could be rendered Lord in the text. (Anytime Lord appears in all capital letters in your Bible, it is translated from the word Jehovah.)

Abraham understood the master-servant relationship,

for he had many servants, one of whom was Eliezer, a slave born into his own household. In the days of Abraham, a bondservant or slave was far better off than a hired servant because his master provided for him totally. It was the master's duty to protect and aid his slave according to his need, even to give him direction in his day-by-day living. Slaves of Hebrews were considered members of the household and thus had a right, after they were circumcised, to participate in the Passover (Exodus 12:43-44). Even if they were gentiles, they were given the rite of circumcision, which brought them under the blessing of the Abrahamic covenant (Genesis 17:10-14).

As you read the following Scriptures ask: What benefits or responsibilities are ours when God is our master? Write them below each verse. (For example, look at Genesis 15:1. Because Abram has the Lord as his master, he need not fear, for the master acts as his shield. The master also rewards his servant. Or look at the next verse, Psalm 123:2—we are to keep our eyes on our master.)

GENESIS 15:1

After these things the word of the LORD came to Abram in a vision, saying, "Do not fear, Abram, I am a shield to you; your reward shall be very great."

PSALM 123:2

Behold, as the eyes of servants look to the hand of their master, as the eyes of a maid to the hand of her mistress; so our eyes look to the LORD our God, until He shall be gracious to us.

PSALM 145:14-16

The LORD sustains all who fall, and raises up all who are bowed down. The eyes of all look to Thee, and Thou dost give them their food in due time. Thou dost open Thy hand, and dost satisfy the desire of every living thing.

PSALM 89:50-51

Remember, O Lord, the reproach of Thy servants; how I do bear in my bosom the reproach of all the many peoples, with which Thine enemies have reproached, O LORD, with which they have reproached the footsteps of Thine anointed.

PSALM 141:8-10

For my eyes are toward Thee, O GOD, the Lord; in Thee I take refuge; do not leave me defenseless. Keep me from the jaws of the trap which they have set for me, and from the snares of those who do iniquity. Let the wicked fall into their own nets, while I pass by safely.

PSALM 119:125

I am Thy servant; give me understanding, that I may know Thy testimonies.

JUDGES 6:14-16

(Gideon calls God "Lord [Adonai].") And the LORD looked at him and said, "Go in this your strength and deliver Israel from the hand of Midian. Have

I not sent you?" And he said to Him, "O Lord, how shall I deliver Israel? Behold, my family is the least in Manasseh, and I am the youngest in my father's house." But the LORD said to him, "Surely I will be with you, and you shall defeat Midian as one man."

Now read the following scriptures and below each one note that over which He is Adonai (Lord). If pertinent, also note the response that is to be given Him as Adonai. Each scripture refers to God as Adonai or Adon.

DEUTERONOMY 9:26

And I prayed to the LORD, and said, "Oh Lord GOD, do not destroy Thy people, even Thine inheritance, whom Thou hast redeemed through Thy greatness, whom Thou hast brought out of Egypt with a mighty hand."

1 KINGS 2:26

Then to Abiathar the priest the king said, "Go to Anathoth to your own field, for you deserve to die; but I will not put you to death at this time, because you carried the ark of the Lord GOD before my father David, and because you were afflicted in everything with which my father was afflicted."

PSALM 2:4

He who sits in the heavens laughs, the Lord scoffs at them.

PSALM 8:1,6-8

O LORD, our Lord, how majestic is Thy name in all the earth, who hast displayed Thy splendor above the heavens! . . . Thou dost make him to rule over the works of Thy hands; Thou hast put all things under his feet, all sheep and oxen, and also the beasts of the field, the birds of the heavens, and the fish of the sea, whatever passes through the paths of the seas.

PSALM 37:12-13

The wicked plots against the righteous, and gnashes at him with his teeth. The Lord laughs at him; for He sees his day is coming.

PSALM 97:5

The mountains melted like wax at the presence of the LORD, at the presence of the Lord of the whole earth.

PSALM 114:7

Tremble, O earth, before the Lord, before the God of Jacob.

PSALM 135:5

For I know that the LORD is great, and that our Lord is above all gods.

PSALM 136:3

Give thanks to the Lord of lords, for His lovingkindness is everlasting.

That's enough for you to meditate upon today. Keep
these questions before you: Can a person really be
saved and deny God's lordship over his life? Can you
call Him 'Lord,' refuse to do the things He tells you to
do, and still go to heaven? It could make all the difference in your understanding of true Christianity.

DAY FOURTEEN

" 'And why do you call Me, "Lord, Lord," and do not
do what I say?' " (Luke 6:46).

" 'And if I am a master, where is My respect?' says
the LORD of hosts to you, O priests who despise My
name . . .' " (Malachi 1:6).

His name is Adonai, Lord, Master. How well His servants have known that down through the ages! Abram
"believed in the LORD; and He reckoned it to him as
righteousness" (Genesis 15:6). The Master had met the
servant's need. He had told Abram how it would be.
Eliezer was not to be Abram's heir, rather, the heir
would come from Abram's own body (Genesis 15:2-6).
Abram would have a seed that would bring salvation
to all the earth. "Now the promises were spoken to
Abraham and to his seed. He does not say, 'And to
seeds,' as referring to many, but rather to one, 'And to
your seed,' that is, Christ" (Galatians 3:16).

Do you see the need to bow before Him and say,
"My Lord"? With submission comes all we need for the
task He puts before us. Whatever it is, as Adonai He
supplies what His servants need in order to perform
their Master's will.

But as Adonai, God has a right to expect obedience. Was this not why God became angry with Moses when He called him to go before Pharaoh and tell him to let God's people go? Listen carefully as Moses speaks to God. (As you read, remember that when *Lord* is in capital letters the word is Jehovah; otherwise the word is Adonai or Adon.)

EXODUS 4:10-14

Then Moses said to the LORD, "Please, Lord, I have never been eloquent, neither recently nor in time past, nor since Thou hast spoken to Thy servant; for I am slow of speech and slow of tongue." And the LORD said to him, "Who has made man's mouth? Or who makes him dumb or deaf, or seeing or blind? Is it not I, the LORD? Now then go, and I, even I, will be with your mouth, and teach you what you are to say." But he said, "Please, Lord, now send *the message* by whomever Thou wilt." Then the anger of the LORD burned against Moses.

Why was God angry? Because Moses was saying, "Lord, Lord [Adonai]," but not trusting and submitting to Him as Adonai. When Isaiah saw God upon His throne, he saw Him as Adonai. "In the year of King Uzziah's death, I saw the Lord sitting on a throne, lofty and exalted, with the train of His robe filling the temple" (Isaiah 6:1). He referred again to Him as Adonai when in verse 8 he said he "heard the voice of the Lord, saying, 'Whom shall I send, and who will go for Us?'" Here the Master is looking for the obedient servant who will say, "Lord, Lord" and do His will. (Note the phrase "who will go for Us," implying a triune God.)

Yet the seraphim declared Him Jehovah-sabaoth, the Lord of hosts, and so Isaiah acknowledged Him as such when he confessed his sin (v.5). Our Lord—our Adonai—is Jehovah, YHWH, and as Jehovah He is to be obeyed. He is God; we are human. He is the

Creator; we are the created, therefore every knee should bow. When Jeremiah was appointed by God to be a prophet to the nations (Jeremiah 1:5), it was Jehovah who appointed him. However, when he responded to God, he addressed Him, "Alas, Lord God!" Jeremiah was literally saying, "Adonai Jehovah." If God is God, then he must be Adonai—He must be Master.

If this is so with God the Father, is it not also with God the Son? Must not God the Son also be Jehovah Adonai? Jesus once asked the Pharisees, "'What do you think about the Christ, whose son is He?' They said to Him, 'The son of David.' He said to them, 'Then how does David in the Spirit call Him "Lord," saying, "THE LORD SAID TO MY LORD, 'SIT AT MY RIGHT HAND, UNTIL I PUT THINE ENEMIES BENEATH THY FEET'"? If David then calls Him "Lord," how is He his son?' And no one was able to answer Him a word, nor did anyone dare from that day on to ask Him another question" (Matthew 22:42-46).

Jesus quoted Psalm 110:1 to prove He was the Son of God. As Jesus quoted the psalm, He also established the fact that He was Adon. The verse reads in the Hebrew, "Jehovah says to my Adon." David was speaking prophetically of the Christ, the Messiah. Remember in Isaiah 6:8 when Jehovah said, "Who will go for Us?" There again we see a reference to the Trinity. Jesus is God, one with the Father (John 10:30-33) and as God, He is Adon, Lord, Master.

For those who have eyes to see, this is the teaching of the New Testament. Over and over Jesus confronted His hearers with His deity and for this the Jews wanted to stone Him. "For a good work we do not stone You, but for blasphemy; and because You, being a man, make Yourself out to be God" (John 10:33).

Many don't mind acknowledging Jesus Christ as a good man, nor even as a prophet, but they do not want to acknowledge Him as God, for if He is God then He must be honored as God.[1] Every knee must bow and confess Him as Lord to the glory of the Father (Philippians 2:10-11).

Jesus' deity and His right to be worshiped as Lord is constantly brought to our attention. And we must make a decision. Two words are translated *Lord* in the New Testament. One is *kurios* and means supreme in authority, controller. This is the most common word used in reference to Jesus Christ. The other is *despotes*, which means an absolute ruler. Read the following scriptures carefully. Below each, write in your own words how these verses show Jesus Christ as Adonai, and what, if anything is required of us.

LUKE 14:25-27

Now great multitudes were going along with Him; and He turned and said to them, "If anyone comes to Me, and does not hate his own father and mother and wife and children and brothers and sisters, yes, and even his own life, he cannot be My disciple. Whoever does not carry his own cross and come after Me cannot be My disciple.

MATTHEW 10:34-40

Do not think that I came to bring peace on the earth; I did not come to bring peace, but a sword. For I came to set A MAN AGAINST HIS FATHER, AND A DAUGHTER AGAINST HER MOTHER, AND A DAUGHTER-IN-LAW AGAINST HER MOTHER-IN-LAW; and A MAN'S ENEMIES WILL BE THE MEMBERS OF HIS HOUSEHOLD. He who loves father or mother more than Me is not worthy of Me; and he who loves son or daughter more than Me is not worthy of Me. And he who does not take his cross and follow after Me is not worthy of Me. He who has found his life shall lose it, and he who has lost his life for My sake shall find it. He who

65

receives you receives Me, and he who receives Me receives Him who sent Me.

JOHN 13:13-16

You call Me Teacher and Lord; and you are right, for so I am. If I then, the Lord and the Teacher, washed your feet, you also ought to wash one another's feet. For I gave you an example that you also should do as I did to you. Truly, truly, I say to you, a slave is not greater than his master; neither is one who is sent greater than the one who sent him.

ROMANS 10:8-10

But what does it say? "THE WORD IS NEAR YOU, IN YOUR MOUTH AND IN YOUR HEART"—that is, the word of faith which we are preaching, that if you confess with your mouth Jesus as Lord, and believe in your heart that God raised Him from the dead, you shall be saved; for with the heart man believes, resulting in righteousness, and with the mouth he confesses, resulting in salvation. (Note what must be confessed for salvation.)

From your study these past two days, answer the following questions:

1. Do you believe Jesus is God?

2. If He is God, is He Adon, Adonai?

3. What do you think it takes to call Jesus "Lord"? What type of commitment does it require on your part?

I want to repeat one scripture from yesterday before we finish our study of Adonai.

MATTHEW 7:21-27

"Not everyone who says to Me, 'Lord, Lord,' will enter the kingdom of heaven; but he who does the will of My Father who is in heaven. Many will say to Me on that day, 'Lord, Lord, did we not prophesy in Your name, and in Your name cast out demons, and in Your name perform many miracles?' And then I will declare to them, 'I never knew you; DEPART FROM ME, YOU WHO PRACTICE LAW-LESSNESS.' Therefore everyone who hears these words of Mine, and acts upon them, may be compared to a wise man, who built his house upon the rock. And the rain descended, and the floods came, and the winds blew, and burst against that house; and yet it did not fall, for it had been founded upon the rock. And everyone who hears these words of Mine, and does not act upon them, will be like a foolish man, who built his house upon the sand. And the rain descended, and the floods came, and the winds blew, and burst against that house; and it fell, and great was its fall."

1. According to this passage, who will enter the kingdom of heaven?

2. How does this pertain to Jesus as Adonai?

3. Can a person deny Jesus' lordship over his life and still go to heaven?

4. Is Jesus Christ your Adonai?

5. Are you a wise or foolish person? How do you know?

"Do you not know that when you present yourselves to someone as slaves for obedience, you are slaves of the one whom you obey, either of sin resulting in death, or of obedience resulting in righteousness? But thanks be to God that though you were slaves of sin, you became obedient from the heart to that form of teaching to which you were committed" (Romans 6:16-17).

Note

1. For additional references to the deity of Jesus Christ, see the following scriptures: John 1:1,14; John 8:24,58; Exodus 3:14; Hebrews 1:1-3,8; Isaiah 9:6-7.

DISCUSSION QUESTIONS FOR DAYS 13 AND 14

1. As you understand it, define the name *Adonai*.

2. What does the lordship of God over a man mean?

3. Why is it important to know God as Adonai before you call on Him as El Shaddai?

4. From your study of the scriptures, explain how the master-servant relationship applies to those who know God as Adonai.

5. What is Jesus' relationship to Adonai?

6. Is Christ Adonai to you?

7. In the light of Jesus Christ being Adonai, how would you explain Matthew 7:21-22 to another?

THE SELF-EXISTENT ONE

DAY FIFTEEN

Of all the names of God, Jehovah is the name most frequently used in the Old Testament. The first of 6,823 usages occurs in Genesis 2:4 where Jehovah is compounded with Elohim.

The name of Jehovah is derived from *havah* which means "to be, to become." Therefore, Jehovah speaks to God's being or essence. Nathan Stone says: "Thus when we read the name Jehovah, or LORD in capital letters, in our Bible, we think in terms of being or existence and life, and we must think of Jehovah as the

Being who is absolutely self existent, the One who in Himself possesses essential life, permanent existence."

At the burning bush, "Moses said to God, 'Behold, I am going to the sons of Israel, and I shall say to them, "The God of your fathers has sent me to you." Now they may say to me, "What is His name?" What shall I say to them?' " (Exodus 3:13).

"And God said to Moses, 'I AM WHO I AM'; and He said, 'Thus you shall say to the sons of Israel, "I AM has sent me to you." ' And God, furthermore, said to Moses, 'Thus you shall say to the sons of Israel, "The LORD, the God of your fathers, the God of Abraham, the God of Isaac, and the God of Jacob, has sent me to you." This is My name forever, and this is My memorial-name to all generations' " (Exodus 3:14-15).

Jehovah is the self-existent One—"I AM WHO I AM." He is the eternal I AM, the Alpha and the Omega, the same yesterday, today, and forever. All of life is contained in Him. Why do we look elsewhere? Why do we not rest in His unchangeableness? He has never failed. Would He begin with me or you? He cannot; He is Jehovah, the self-existent, covenant-keeping God.

When God said this to Moses, His people understood for the first time the significance of what Jehovah meant. Although *Jehovah* was used as early as Genesis 2:4, it wasn't until His revelation to Moses that they understood that this was the name that went with His covenant promise to His people. Exodus 6:2-4 says, "I am the LORD [Jehovah]; and I appeared to Abraham, Isaac, and Jacob, as God Almighty [El Shaddai], but by My name, LORD [Jehovah], I did not make Myself known to them. And I also established My covenant with them, to give them the land of Canaan, the land in which they sojourned."

Jehovah fulfilled the covenant He had made with Abraham regarding the land of Canaan, and, therefore, the Israelites returned to Canaan after four hundred years of bondage in Egypt (Genesis 15:13-21). God reveals Himself to His covenant people as the unchanging God who remains faithful to His word throughout many generations.

When you need assurance that God is there, keeping His promises, never changing even though you have wavered in your promises to Him, run to your Jehovah. Trust in His name. It can't change because He can't change. He is Jehovah, the same yesterday, today, and forever.

"And the LORD [Jehovah] descended in the cloud and stood there with him [Moses] as he called upon the name of the LORD [Jehovah]. Then the LORD [Jehovah] passed by in front of him and proclaimed, 'The LORD [Jehovah], the LORD [Jehovah] God, compassionate and gracious, slow to anger, and abounding in lovingkindness and truth; who keeps lovingkindness[2] for thousands, who forgives iniquity, transgression and sin; yet He will by no means leave *the guilty* unpunished, visiting the iniquity of fathers on the children and on the grandchildren to the third and fourth generations'" (Exodus 34:5-7). This is your Jehovah!

So that you will remember these adjectives which are used in connection with *Jehovah*, list them below. When you finish, write out a prayer of praise and worship to your Jehovah.

O Father, as Moses prayed, so we pray, show us Your glory! As You descended in the cloud, stood with Moses, and proclaimed Your name, will You not pass by us in all Your goodness, proclaiming Your name? O Lord, we want to know You . . . by name.

Note
   1. Lovingkindness is a covenant term.

1. Jehovah is used for God more than any other name. Exactly what does Jehovah mean?

2. How does the meaning of Jehovah parallel with God's answer to Moses in Exodus 3:13-15?

3. How is Jehovah usually translated in the Old Testament?

4. Jehovah is the God of the covenant. From your study, what did you learn about your covenant-keeping Jehovah that can be applied to your life today?

THE
LORD
WILL PROVIDE

Day Sixteen

O Jehovah, our self-existent One, You who possesses essential life, who am I that You are mindful of me? If You are the all-sufficient One, why do You need me, why do You want me? And what have I to offer You?

He needs and wants you because He is more than Jehovah. He is *Jehovah-jireh, Jehovah-tsidkenu, Jehovah-nissi, Jehovah-raah, Jehovah-rapha, Jehovah-shalom, Jehovah-sabaoth, Jehovah-shammah, Jehovah-mekoddishkem.* And what do these names mean? Each one of them compounded with Jehovah shows us that the very essence of His Being is to love, to give, to be more than self-constrained. As the self-existent one, He desires to meet the needs of those He created in His own image. Thus, He becomes Jehovah our provider, Jehovah our shepherd, Jehovah that sanctifies us, and so on. To be beyond Himself is part of His character and, as you and I take on His character more and more, we then reach out beyond ourselves to manifest to others what He is to us.

The first of these compound "Jehovah" names we will look at is *Jehovah-jireh*, "the Lord will provide." The usage of this name in the life of Abraham is very significant. But before we study it, I want you to glean what you can on your own. Therefore, your assignment today is to read a passage from Genesis. As you read, give yourself time for meditation, asking God to help you understand His truth and have your faith strengthened. As you read Genesis 22:1-19 look for the following:

1. Underline "The Lord will provide." This is His Jehovah-jireh.

2. Note or mark the words *love, obey,* and *worship* in some way.

This is the first mention of these three words in the Bible. God has written twenty-one chapters and until now these words have not been used. When a significant word is mentioned for the first time in the Word of God, the principles connected with that word hold true throughout the rest of Scripture. This is called the principle of first mention.

GENESIS 22:1-19

Now it came about after these things, that God tested Abraham, and said to him, "Abraham!" And he said, "Here I am." And He said, "Take now your son, your only son, whom you love, Isaac, and go to the land of Moriah; and offer him there as a burnt offering on one of the mountains of which I will tell you." So Abraham rose early in the morning and saddled his donkey, and took two of his young men with him and Isaac his son; and he split wood for the burnt offering, and arose and went to the place of which God had told him. On the third day Abraham raised his eyes and saw the place from a distance. And Abraham said to his young men, "Stay here with the donkey, and I and the lad will go yonder; and we will worship and return to you." And Abraham took the wood of the burnt offering and laid it on Isaac his son, and he took in his hand the fire and the knife. So the two of them walked on together. And Isaac spoke to Abraham his father and said, "My father!" And he said, "Here I am, my son." And he said, "Behold, the fire and the wood, but where is the lamb for the burnt offering?" And Abraham said, "God will provide for Himself the lamb for the burnt offering, my son." So the two of them walked on together. Then they came to the place of which God had told him; and Abraham built the altar there, and arranged the wood, and bound his son Isaac, and laid him on the altar on top of the wood. And Abraham stretched out his hand, and took the knife to slay his son. But the angel of the LORD called to him from heaven, and said, "Abraham, Abraham!" And he said, "Here I am." And he said, "Do not stretch out your hand against the lad, and do nothing to him; for now I know that you fear God, since you have not withheld your son, your only son, from Me." Then Abraham raised his eyes and looked, and behold, behind *him* a ram caught in the thicket by his horns; and Abraham went and took the ram, and offered him up for a burnt offering in the place of his

son. And Abraham called the name of that
place The LORD Will Provide, as it is said to this
day, "In the mount of the LORD it will be provided." Then the angel of the LORD called to
Abraham a second time from heaven, and said,
"By Myself I have sworn," declares the LORD,
"because you have done this thing, and have
not withheld your son, your only son, indeed I
will greatly bless you, and I will greatly multiply your seed as the stars of the heavens, and
as the sand which is on the seashore; and your
seed shall possess the gate of their enemies.
And in your seed all the nations of the earth
shall be blessed, because you have obeyed My
voice." So Abraham returned to his young men,
and they arose and went together to
Beersheba; and Abraham lived at Beersheba.

In the light of what you saw regarding Jehovah-
jireh and the words love, obey, and worship, write out
what you have learned. Write out the events and circumstances surrounding the use of each word and any
other significant insights into the usage of the word or
its timing in history. An example of this is found at the
end of Genesis 22:1-19 where you see love first used
in connection with a father and his only son.

Love: (Used in connection with a father and his
only son.)

Obey:

Worship:

Now read Genesis 22:1-19 again. See if these three words in any way give you a picture of Jesus Christ and His work on your behalf. Hint: Compare this use of love with John 3:16. If you don't get finished today, then we will work on it some more tomorrow.

May our Father richly bless you through what you see.

DAY SEVENTEEN

Today, begin by again reading Genesis 22:1-19, then answer the following questions:

1. Why was Abraham going to offer up his son?

2. In what land would he make the sacrifice?

3. Where in that land would the sacrifice be made?

4. Why did Abraham name that place "The Lord Will Provide" (Jehovah-jireh)?

5. Finish any insights you still need to record on the words love, obey, and worship.

6. What is the order of these three words in Genesis 22:1-19? Do you see any possible reason for this order? What is the relationship among the three words?

7. Why did God tell Abraham to offer up Isaac?

8. What did Abraham offer to God in Isaac's place?

9. Do you deserve to die for your sins?

10. What did God provide in your place?

11. Who was Jesus to God?

Think on all this. Talk to your Father about it, and we will discuss it tomorrow.

DAY EIGHTEEN

When Cesare Borgia came face to face with death, he cried, "When I lived, I provided for everything but death; now I must die, and I am unprovided to die."

Unprovided to die. Why? Because Cesare Borgia had failed to call upon the name of the Lord. He had refused to believe and obey God's Word that "WHOEVER WILL CALL UPON THE NAME OF THE LORD WILL BE SAVED" (Romans 10:13).

People can, within limits, provide for everything while they live, but they can't provide for death. For death there is only one provider, Jehovah-jireh. Jehovah, who in Himself possesses essential life, is the only One who can make provision for us as sinners to live. He did so by providing us with the Lamb of God that takes away the sins of the world. "For just as the Father raises the dead and gives them life, even so the

Son also gives life to whom He wishes" (John 5:21).

How fitting it is, then, that the first time we see God as our Jehovah-jireh, we see a father offering his only son on Mount Moriah. Love, worship, and obedience become three in one!

And what was so significant about Mount Moriah besides being the place where Abraham offered Isaac? Second Chronicles 3:1 tells us: "Then Solomon began to build the house of the LORD in Jerusalem on Mount Moriah, where the LORD had appeared to his father David, at the place that David had prepared, on the threshing floor of Ornan the Jebusite."

From then on at Mount Moriah every temple sacrifice for sin would echo Abraham's words, "The LORD Will Provide [Jehovah-jireh], as it is said to this day, 'In the mount of the LORD it will be provided' " (Genesis 22:14). Every lamb, every goat, every sacrifice would point to the one ultimate sacrifice.

Since it is impossible for the blood of bulls and goats to take away sins, God prepared a body for His Son (Hebrews 10:4-5). Then, at the appointed time, on the day of the Passover, Jehovah took that Son, His only Son whom He loved, and led Him to Mount Calvary. There He laid Him on the cross. This time there was no voice from heaven to stop the hand of death; there was no ram in the thicket to take His place, for this Lamb was the only provision of Jehovah-jireh for the sins of the world. What man could not provide, Jehovah-jireh did!

Have you, Beloved, gone to Jehovah-jireh and obtained by faith the provision for your sins, for your death? Or will you echo Cesare Borgia's cry, "Now I must die, and I am unprovided to die"?

Die you must, "It is appointed unto men once to die" (Hebrews 9:27, KJV). "He who believes in the Son has eternal life; but he who does not obey the Son shall not see life, but the wrath of God abides on him" (John 3:36).

What will it be? Life or death? What provision has been made for your sins? Will it satisfy God? Write your answers below.

DAY NINETEEN

Was eternal life all that Jehovah provided? No, not if you think of eternal life as life after death, because we have yet to live this life. There is much we need in order to be more than conquerors.

The word for provide, *jireh*, in the Old Testament is literally "to see." But how do Hebrew scholars get "provide" out of it? Because He is God, when He sees, He foresees. Our all-knowing, ever-present, eternal Father knows the end from the beginning and thus, in His omniscience, He provides. Therefore, when Abraham responded in Genesis 22:8, "God will provide for Himself the lamb for the burnt offering, my son," he was literally saying, "God will see for Himself the lamb." The word *see* denotes provision, for when "Abraham raised his eyes and looked . . . behold . . . behind him a ram caught in the thicket by his horns" (Genesis 22:13). Because of God's provision, Abraham named that place: "The LORD Will Provide [Jehovah-jireh], as it is said to this day. 'In the mount of the LORD it will be provided' " or literally "it will be seen" (Genesis 22:14).

I don't want you to miss this precious truth. I want you to know all that it means to call upon your Jehovah-jireh, for He provides more than your salvation. Not only has Jehovah foreseen your need for salvation and made provision through the death and resurrection of His Son, but He also sees your day-by-day needs. That is why Jesus instructed: "And when you are praying, do not use meaningless repetition, as the Gentiles do, for they suppose that they will be heard for their many words. Therefore do not be like them; for your Father knows what you need, before you ask Him" (Matthew 6:7-8).

Yes, our Father, Jehovah-jireh, sees our needs and so knows them, yet He instructs us to pray, "Give us this day our daily bread" (Matthew 6:11).

Do you feel silly asking God for bread when you can get it yourself? Do you feel that it is unnecessary to come to the sovereign Ruler of the universe with the seeming trivia of your individual needs? Do you wonder why God would even bother with you anyway?

O Beloved, our God, our Jehovah-jireh is bidding us to come. We are coming to the one who is for us. "He who did not spare His own Son, but delivered Him up for us all, how will He not also with Him freely give us all things?" (Romans 8:32). "In the mount of the LORD it will be provided" (Genesis 22:14). At Calvary, through the death and resurrection of Jesus Christ, "my God shall supply all your needs according to His riches in glory in Christ Jesus" (Philippians 4:19).

He is a God who is for you, not against you. In any test you can lay your Isaac on the altar. You can worship Jehovah-jireh in obedience and know that whatever you need, the Lord will provide it.

Whatever your circumstances, where are you to go for provision?

"Woe to those who go down to Egypt for help, and rely on horses, and trust in chariots because they are many, and in horsemen because they are very strong, but they do not look to the Holy One of Israel, nor seek the LORD!" (Isaiah 31:1).

DISCUSSION QUESTIONS FOR DAYS 16 THROUGH 19

1. Why is it significant that the name Jehovah is combined with other words that describe God's character?

2. The name Jehovah-jireh is translated, "The Lord will provide." How is this quality of His nature manifested in the account of Abraham and Isaac?

3. Thinking back over the account of Abraham and Isaac on Mount Moriah, what was the order of the three key words: *obey, love,* and *worship?* Why is the order significant?

4. Why do you think God asked Abraham to slay Isaac as a sacrifice?

5. What has God asked you to do that was as difficult for you as sacrificing Isaac must have been for Abraham? Why do you think He required that of you?

6. Briefly, how has Jehovah-jireh provided for our "deaths?" What sacrifice has He made for us?

7. What is the meaning of the Old Testament word *jireh?*

8. How is that ability of God to foresee pertinent to your life?

9. When you have any need, what can you expect from Jehovah-jireh?

10. Recall a time in your walk with Jehovah-jireh when He met your need. Tell the group.

THE
LORD
WHO HEALS

Our wounds are great. As sin ravaged Christ's body at Calvary, so it has ravaged men, women, and children. Multitudes are drained, poured out like water; nothing seems in place. All their bones are out of joint; their hearts are gone, melted like wax. There is not fight nor energy left within them, for their strength is dried up like clay; the ability, the freedom to communicate is lost. They are laid down in the dust of the earth (see Psalm 22:14-15). In their misery there are very few to comfort them; rather they seem surrounded by enemies. Evildoers encompass them, staring with curiosity at their misery, not having pity but seeking only to use them to their advantage in order to divide the spoils of their lives (Psalm 22:16-18).

Am I being melodramatic? Am I exaggerating? I wish I were. I wish it were not as grave as I say. But it is, and more. However, if I were to describe it as it really is, in all probability some of you would not read any further. We don't want to hear it. We don't want to know it. The stark reality of our sin is too sickening, too unpleasant. We want to shut our eyes, stop our ears, and bury our heads. Ignorance is bliss: we live in our own world, undisturbed, uninformed, and untroubled by realities that would otherwise demand our concern and attention as God's ambassadors of reconciliation. It is a delight to be an ambassador if all it involves is notoriety and privileges and the niceties of life; but bring on the demands of resolving issues and problems, of confronting the unpleasant and the unjust, and we say, "You can forget being an ambassador."

We ourselves want to be healed, but we do not want to be involved in healing others. We don't want our hands soiled. Let us send our money; let us give from afar. Let us hear only enough to motivate us to compassion but not to recurrent dreams that haunt us.

If we are to be God's representatives on earth, manifesting to the world the character of God, if we are to minister rather than be ministered unto, we must search out those who need a physician and become actively involved in healing the wounds of His people. Unquestionably, Beloved; for the name of our God is Jehovah-rapha, the Lord who heals!

DAY TWENTY-ONE

"Is there no balm in Gilead? Is there no physician there?" Jeremiah 8:22.

Yes, there is a balm in Gilead. There is a physician

there. His name is Jehovah-rapha, the Lord who heals. But how many know His name? What does it mean? What does He heal? Physical infirmities? Illnesses of mind, of soul? Spiritual wounds or physical wounds? These are some of the questions we will seek to answer as we search Scripture in order to know "what saith the Lord."

The longer Israel journeyed with God, the more familiar she became with His character and ways. The revelation was progressive. When her deliverance from Egypt came, she fully understood why He was called Jehovah. For it was Jehovah who heard her cry and remembered the covenant He had made with Abraham (Genesis 15:13-21; Exodus 3:7-8; 16:2-4). Through that deliverance they also saw Him as Jehovah-jireh, for once again, through sacrifice, God provided what they needed. It was the Passover Lamb that bought their release from slavery under Pharaoh.

Even though released from Egypt (a picture of the world), God's people still bore some of Egypt's ways. The stench of Egypt was unmistakably discernible when the winds of testing blew. Israel came to know God in another light. The incident occurred soon after the marvelous deliverance from the pursuing Egyptians at the Red Sea.

Read Exodus 15:22-27 below and answer the questions that follow:

EXODUS 15:22-27

Then Moses led Israel from the Red Sea, and they went out into the wilderness of Shur; and they went three days in the wilderness and found no water. And when they came to Marah, they could not drink the waters of Marah, for they were bitter; therefore it was named Marah. So the people grumbled at Moses, saying, "What shall we drink?" Then he cried out to the LORD, and the LORD showed him a tree; and he threw *it* into the waters, and the waters became sweet. There He made for them a statute and regulation, and there He tested them. And He said, "If you will give earnest heed to the voice of the LORD your God, and do what is right in His sight, and give ear to His commandments, and keep all His statutes, I will put none of the diseases on you which I have put on the Egyptians; for I, the LORD, am your healer." Then they came to Elim where there *were* twelve springs of water and seventy date palms, and they camped there beside the waters.

1. What was Moses' cure for the bitter waters of Marah?

2. How did the people happen to end up at Marah? Was it an accident? Read Exodus 13:21-22.

3. Do you think the bitter waters of Marah were an accident, a result of poor leadership, a surprise? Why do you think this?

4. Besides bitter waters being made sweet by a tree, what else happened at Marah?

5. What would keep the people healthy?

6. Who put the diseases on whom? Why do you think He did?

7. Who would do the healing? How does this compare with Deuteronomy 32:39? Isaiah 45:6-7?

8. What kind of disease does Jehovah-rapha heal?

Jehovah-rapha heals . . . but what does He heal? Below are some scriptures on healing that are far from exhaustive but which should help you answer this question. Read each one carefully seeking God's revelation, and then write out what you learn about healing from that passage.

Before you begin, let me say that the Old Testament passages will contain the Hebrew word *rapha*, "to heal." Of course, the New Testament word for *heal* will be different because the New Testament was written in Greek. Remember, also, as you look at New Testament passages, that Jesus is God, one with the Father. "Whatever the Father does, these things the Son also does in like manner" (John 5:19).

SCRIPTURES ON HEALING	WHAT I LEARNED ABOUT HEALING
2 KINGS 20:1,4-5 In those days Hezekiah became mortally ill. And Isaiah the prophet the son	

WHAT I LEARNED
ABOUT HEALING

of Amoz came to him and
said to him, "Thus says the
LORD, 'Set your house in
order, for you shall die and
not live' " . . . the word of
the LORD came to him
[Isaiah], saying, "Return
and say to Hezekiah the
leader of My people, 'Thus
says the LORD, the God of
your father David, "I have
heard your prayer, I have
seen your tears; behold, I
will heal you. On the third
day you shall go up to the
house of the LORD." ' "

2 CHRONICLES 7:14

[If] My people who are
called by My name humble
themselves and pray, and
seek My face and turn from
their wicked ways, then I
will hear from heaven, will
forgive their sin, and will
heal their land.

ISAIAH 19:22; 53:5

And the LORD will strike
Egypt, striking but heal-
ing; so they will return to
the LORD, and He will
respond to them and will
heal them. . . . But He
was pierced through for
our transgressions, He
was crushed for our iniq-

uities; the chastening for
our well-being *fell* upon
Him, and by His scourg-
ing we are healed.

JEREMIAH 30:15-17
"Why do you cry out over
your injury? Your pain is
incurable. Because your
iniquity is great and your
sins are numerous, I have
done these things to you.
Therefore all who devour
you shall be devoured; and
all your adversaries, every
one of them, shall go into
captivity; and those who
plunder you shall be for
plunder, and all who prey
upon you I will give for
prey. For I will restore you
to health and I will heal
you of your wounds,"
declares the LORD, "Because
they have called you an
outcast, saying: 'It is Zion;
no one cares for her.'"

PSALM 147:3
He heals the broken-
hearted, and binds up their
wounds.

PSALM 103:1-3
Bless the LORD, O my soul;
and all that is within me,
bless His holy name. Bless

the LORD, O my soul, and forget none of His benefits; who pardons all your iniquities; who heals all your diseases.

MATTHEW 8:16-17

And when evening had come, they brought to Him many who were demon-possessed; and He cast out the spirits with a word, and healed all who were ill in order that what was spoken through Isaiah the prophet might be fulfilled, saying, "HE HIMSELF TOOK OUR INFIRMITIES, AND CARRIED AWAY OUR DISEASES." (Note when Isaiah 53:4 was fulfilled.)

LUKE 4:18

"THE SPIRIT OF THE LORD IS UPON ME, BECAUSE HE ANOINTED ME TO PREACH THE GOSPEL TO THE POOR. HE HAS SENT ME TO PROCLAIM RELEASE TO THE CAPTIVES, AND RECOVERY OF SIGHT TO THE BLIND, TO SET FREE THOSE WHO ARE DOWNTRODDEN, TO PROCLAIM THE FAVORABLE YEAR OF THE LORD."

1 PETER 2:24-25

And He Himself bore our sins in His body on the cross, that we might die to sin and live to righteousness; for by His wounds you were healed. For you were continually straying like sheep, but now you have returned to the Shepherd and Guardian of your souls. (Parallel with Isaiah 53:5-6.)

Below, write a summary statement on what Jehovah-rapha heals.

Are you wounded? Do you need a physician? Is there a balm in Gilead? Have you asked Him to heal you? "Heal me, O LORD, and I will be healed; save me and I will be saved, for Thou art my praise" (Jeremiah 17:14).

DAY TWENTY-THREE

I will never forget the day I was saved. The night before I'd been at a party. The only thing I remember about that night was a man named Jim who looked at me and said, "Why don't you quit telling God what you want and tell Him that Jesus Christ is all you need?" His words irritated me.

"Jesus Christ is not all I need." My reply was curt. "I need a husband, I need a . . ." and one by one I enumerated my needs, emphasizing each one by numbering them on my fingers. At five, I considered that I had surely proven my case, so with that I turned on my heels and went home.

For some time I had realized my life-style was unacceptable to God. I knew that were I to stand before God, I would hear Him rightfully say, "Depart from Me." My sins were obvious, and even I could not excuse them. For the first time in my life I had seen my poverty of spirit. Although I had tried, I could not quit sinning. Nothing good dwelt in my flesh, and I knew it (Romans 7:18-20). I had made resolution after resolution to be good, to stop being immoral, only to give in again and again. Finally, I concluded that there was no way I could ever be set free; I just wasn't strong enough spiritually to change. I knew I was sick—sick of soul. As a registered nurse I was an active participant in the healing of many bodies, but I didn't know of any doctor who could heal my soul. And heal myself? Well, it was impossible. I had tried.

After my divorce I lived with gnawing guilt until finally my sin became an acceptable way of life. After all, how could my friends condemn me? We all lived the same way! Some days I even thought, *If I could just be born again . . . have another start at life.* Then I would dream of what-could-have-been-if-only! I didn't know the term "born again" was in the Bible. Although my family was very religious, the Bible had not been a major part of my life. For the most part I didn't know what God's Word said. By this time, I had lived for twenty-nine years, and no one had ever asked me when or even if I had been saved. I had never heard an invitation for salvation, nor had I realized that it isn't church membership or being good that makes us Christians.

Heaven and hell? Hell was what you made of your life here on earth. Heaven? Well, if my good deeds outweighed my bad, surely I would make it. At least that was what I was told! To be honest, I never felt that nice people were in any danger. No one around me had a burden for the lost. I had never heard a sermon on the need to witness.

When the morning of July 16, 1963, dawned, I couldn't face going to work. I called the doctor for whom I worked and told him I was sick and that I would see him Monday. I hung up the phone and got Tommy off to day camp. At loose ends, I decided I'd bake a cake and then take the boys camping. Suddenly, in the middle of the kitchen, I looked at Mark, hungry for love, hanging on to my skirt, and said, "Mommy's got to be alone for a few minutes." With that I rushed upstairs to my bedroom and threw myself on the floor beside my bed. "O God, I don't care what you do to me, I don't care if I never see another man as long as I live, I don't care if you paralyze me from the neck down, I don't care what you do to my two boys, if you'll just give me peace!"

There beside my bed I found that there is a balm in Gilead that heals the sin-sick soul. There is a Great Physician. His name is Jehovah-rapha, although I would first come to know Him as the Lord Jesus Christ, the Prince of Peace. On that day in my bedroom He applied the cross to the bitter waters of my life and I was healed of sin's mortal wounds (Galatians 3:13-14; 1 Peter 2:24). I had turned to Jehovah-rapha, returning to the Shepherd and Guardian of my soul (1 Peter 2:25).

Only one Physician can heal the ills of our souls. Why look elsewhere? Why not trust in the name of our Lord and rely on God (Isaiah 50:10)?

Where do you run when you need healing? He is there, our Jehovah-rapha—waiting with outstretched arms, Calvary arms.

Day Twenty-Four

Health, healing, and obedience, according to Exodus 15:26, go together. As you read listen carefully to the Spirit of God: "And He said, 'If you will give earnest heed to the voice of the LORD your God, and do what is right in His sight, and give ear to His commandments, and keep all His statutes, I will put none of the diseases on you which I have put on the Egyptians; for I, the LORD, am your healer.'"

Like it or not, there is a direct correlation between sin and sickness. Not just sickness of body, but also of spirit and soul. And according to Exodus 15:26, which you just read, and the scriptures you studied two days ago, God is as active in wounding as He is in healing. Did you note "I will put none of the diseases on you which I have put on the Egyptians"?

Now, I imagine that you are wondering if I am saying that all sickness is due to sin. I have to answer that in two ways, so hear me carefully. First, if man had not sinned there would be no sickness; so in a sense all sickness is due to sin. However, I don't believe that all physical or emotional illness is a consequence of personal sin. I believe some illnesses have other causes. Let me share with you a few scriptures that can throw some biblical light on this. Although they won't be exhaustive, I believe the exercise will be of benefit. Then when we finish, I want to discuss the way to deal with sickness of body, soul, and spirit.

As you read each scripture, note once again in your own words what you learn about sickness, especially in regard to sin. Is sickness always due to personal sin? Did sin cause the sickness? If so, whose sin?

SCRIPTURE   **YOUR ANALYSIS**

David had sinned and numbered the children of Israel (1 Chronicles 21:8, 17):

96

SCRIPTURE	YOUR ANALYSIS

1 CHRONICLES 21:10-14

"Go and speak to David, saying, 'Thus says the LORD, "I offer you three things; choose for yourself one of them, that I may do *it* to you." ' " So Gad came to David and said to him, "Thus says the LORD, 'Take for yourself either three years of famine, or three months to be swept away before your foes, while the sword of your enemies overtakes *you*, or else three days of the sword of the LORD, even pestilence in the land, and the angel of the LORD destroying throughout all the territory of Israel.' Now, therefore, consider what answer I shall return to Him who sent me." And David said to Gad, "I am in great distress; please let me fall into the hand of the LORD, for His mercies are very great. But do not let me fall into the hand of man." So the LORD sent a pestilence on Israel; 70,000 men of Israel fell.

NUMBERS 12:9-13

So the anger of the LORD burned against them and He departed. But when the cloud had withdrawn from

SCRIPTURE	YOUR ANALYSIS

over the tent, behold, Miriam *was* leprous, as *white* as snow. As Aaron turned toward Miriam, behold, she *was* leprous. Then Aaron said to Moses, "Oh, my lord, I beg you, do not account *this* sin to us, in which we have acted foolishly and in which we have sinned. Oh, do not let her be like one dead, whose flesh is half eaten away when he comes from his mother's womb!" And Moses cried out to the LORD, saying, "O God, heal her, I pray!"

PSALM 38:1-3

O LORD, rebuke me not in Thy wrath; and chasten me not in Thy burning anger. For Thine arrows have sunk deep into me, and Thy hand has pressed down on me. There is no soundness in my flesh because of Thine indignation; there is no health in my bones because of my sin.

ISAIAH 1:4-6

Alas, sinful nation, people weighed down with iniquity, offspring of evildoers, sons who act corruptly! They have abandoned the LORD, they have despised the Holy One of Israel, they have turned away from Him. Where will you be stricken again, *as* you continue in *your* rebellion? The whole head is sick, and the whole heart is faint. From the sole of the foot even to the head there is nothing sound in it, *only* bruises, welts, and raw wounds, not pressed out or bandaged, nor softened with oil.

JOHN 9:1-3
And as He passed by, He saw a man blind from birth. And His disciples asked Him, saying, "Rabbi, who sinned, this man or his parents, that he should be born blind?" Jesus answered, "*It was* neither *that* this man sinned, nor his parents; but *it was* in order that the works of God might be displayed in him."

JOHN 5:5-8,14
And a certain man was there, who had been thirty-eight years in his sickness. When Jesus saw him lying there, and knew that he had already been a long time *in that condition,* He said to him, "Do you wish

to get well?" The sick man answered Him, "Sir, I have no man to put me into the pool when the water is stirred up, but while I am coming, another steps down before me." Jesus said to him, "Arise, take up your pallet, and walk." . . . Afterward Jesus found him in the temple, and said to him, "Behold, you have become well; do not sin anymore, so that nothing worse may befall you."

1 CORINTHIANS 11:27-32
Therefore whoever eats the bread or drinks the cup of the Lord in an unworthy manner, shall be guilty of the body and the blood of the Lord. But let a man examine himself, and so let him eat of the bread and drink of the cup. For he who eats and drinks, eats and drinks judgment to himself, if he does not judge the body rightly. For this reason many among you are weak and sick, and a number sleep. But if we judged ourselves rightly, we should not be judged. But when we are judged, we are disciplined by the Lord in order that we may

not be condemned along with the world.

PHILIPPIANS 2:25-30

But I thought it necessary to send to you Epaphroditus, my brother and fellow worker and fellow soldier, who is also your messenger and minister to my need; because he was longing for you all and was distressed because you had heard that he was sick. For indeed he was sick to the point of death, but God had mercy on him, and not on him only but also on me, lest I should have sorrow upon sorrow. Therefore I have sent him all the more eagerly in order that when you see him again you may rejoice and I may be less concerned *about you*. Therefore receive him in the Lord with all joy, and hold men like him in high regard; because he came close to death for the work of Christ, risking his life to complete what was deficient in your service to me.

1 TIMOTHY 5:22-25

Do not lay hands upon anyone *too* hastily and thus

share *responsibility for* the sins of others; keep yourself free from sin. No longer drink water *exclusively,* but use a little wine for the sake of your stomach and your frequent ailments. The sins of some men are quite evident, going before them to judgment; for others, their *sins* follow after. Likewise also, deeds that are good are quite evident, and those which are otherwise cannot be concealed.

JAMES 5:14-16

Is anyone among you sick? Let him call for the elders of the church, and let them pray over him, anointing him with oil in the name of the Lord; and the prayer offered in faith will restore the one who is sick, and the Lord will raise him up, and if he has committed sins, they will be forgiven him. Therefore confess your sins to one another, and pray for one another, so that you may be healed. The effective prayer of a righteous man can accomplish much.

That, Beloved, is enough for you to meditate on today. Have you gained any insights into why so many are hurting, wounded, and in despair? If so, write them below.

DAY TWENTY-FIVE

Where do people turn when they need healing? Isn't it usually to other people? And when people turn to you for help, how do you deal with them? Your answer is essential, for it could make the difference between life and death, physically or spiritually. It could also make the difference between oppression and bondage, peace and freedom.

So often people come to us at Precept Ministries seeking our counsel. Many have already been counseled, but to no avail. Sometimes the counseling has been ineffective because the counselee simply would not walk in obedience to godly counsel.

Often, however, that is not the case. In many instances we find that the counselor has evidently failed to deal with the spiritual problem. He has not sought wisdom from Jehovah-rapha nor asked Him for His diagnosis. He has not probed to see if there is sin that needs to be dealt with. Frequently we find that the counselor has not opened the medicine of God's Word and applied it to the subject's wounds.

Not too long ago we dealt with a man who had been involved in homosexuality. Although he had cried out for deliverance, he was still approached and propositioned by other men. He had received what some would consider the best of counsel from great theologians. Yet, never once did those counselors discern the demonic powers at work in him. His tears were almost bitter. Was he to fight this battle for the rest of his days?

As we prayed and counseled this young man, God showed us what the problem was. Quietly and simply we claimed what was ours because of Calvary and because of our completeness in Christ Jesus. Then we took our authority over the enemy. Our friend has a new radiance about him—his masculinity shows. He writes, "God has used you to set me free from the awful bondage of a lifetime. The changes in my life have been nothing less than dramatic. The restlessness is gone, the constant depression and suicidal thoughts have disappeared. The constant lust is gone. I can also look in the mirror without this intense feeling of hate taking over. I actually feel good about myself now."

It is not shameful to admit your need of healing. Until you do, there really can be none. Jesus said, "It is not those who are healthy who need a physician, but those who are ill. But go and learn what this means, 'I DESIRE COMPASSION, AND NOT SACRIFICE,' for I did not come to call the righteous, but sinners" (Matthew 9:12-13).

Whether his illness is physical, emotional, or spiritual, a person should first seek healing from Jehovah-rapha. Second Chronicles 16:12 says: "And in the thirty-ninth year of his reign Asa became diseased in his feet. His disease was severe, yet even in his disease he did not seek the LORD but the physicians."

Whether it is the illness of a nation or of a single human being, by now you have seen that our need for healing can be because of the sin of a people, a leader, or an individual. It is God who heals lands, pestilences, wars, bodies, emotions, souls, spirits. Oh, He may and often does use us as His instrument of healing, yet the instrument is powerless without the Physician's power. Therefore, at the risk of seeming

redundant, let me say again: Whenever you need healing, first consult Jehovah-rapha. Second, when seeking
healing, explore whether sin is involved as the cause
of the problem.

Do you remember when I said that we must admit
our need of healing of spirit, soul, or body, but until
we do there can really be no healing? Sin affects our
spirits, and the spirit can cause sickness of our emotions and our bodies. David wrote, "I am full of anxi-
ety because of my sin" (Psalm 38:18). Sin may not
always be the cause of the problem; in fact, personal
sin may not even be a contributing factor. However,
we should pray: "Search me, O God, and know my
heart; try me and know my anxious thoughts; and see
if there be any hurtful [wicked] way in me, and lead
me in the everlasting way" (Psalm 139:23-24). Paul
wrote, "I am conscious of nothing against myself, yet I
am not by this acquitted; but the one who examines
me is the Lord" (1 Corinthians 4:4). It's wise to have
God search our hearts.

If sin is discovered, we must deal with it thoroughly.
Not to do so can stay the healing hand of God and
even bring further illness. "He who conceals his transgressions will not prosper, but he who confesses and
forsakes *them* will find compassion. How blessed is
the man who fears always, but he who hardens his
heart will fall into calamity" (Proverbs 28:13-14). God
always meets us at the point of our obedience and
there He comes over to our side. In Psalm 103:3, "pardons all your iniquities" comes before "heals all your
diseases."

I could say so much more about the issue of sin;
however, neither time nor space permits that now.[1] Let
me simply finish our study on Jehovah-rapha with a
few questions and a precious scripture. Write your
answers.

The Lord Who Heals

1. Do you fear (reverence) your God as Jehovah-rapha?

2. Have you realized that the One who heals is also the One who must judge sin, even in the life of a child of God who will not judge it himself?

3. When you pray for your country asking God to heal your land, do you realize that first you must turn from your wicked ways (2 Chronicles 7:14)?

4. When you counsel others, do you take them to Jehovah-rapha, or do you try to heal them yourself? Why?

5. Is there no balm in Gilead, no Jehovah-rapha there?

"But for you who fear My name the sun of righteousness will rise with healing in its wings" (Malachi 4:2).

"Heal me, O LORD, and I will be healed; save me and I will be saved, for Thou art my praise" (Jeremiah 17:14).

Note

1. I have dealt wih the topic of sin thoroughly along with many other topics in my daily devotional book, *How Can I Live. A Devotional Journey with Kay Arthur* (Old Tappan, N.J.: Fleming H. Revell, 1982).

DISCUSSION QUESTIONS FOR DAYS 20 THROUGH 25

1. What is the meaning of the name, Jehovah-rapha?

2. From the scriptures that you have studied, what can you conclude about the type of healing that Jehovah-rapha performs?

3. In the study of Jehovah-rapha, what correlation between sin and sickness did you discover?

4. What does God say regarding the judgment of sin in your own life? What does your own judgment of sin in your life eliminate? (See 1 Corinthians 11:27-32).

5. Where is one to go for healing—whether physical, spiritual, or emotional healing? Are there any exceptions?

6. Think about the last time you needed to be healed. To whom did you go? What happened? (Let someone share this experience if they would like.)

7. Read Malachi 4:2 and Jeremiah 17:14. What do you see in these two verses that apparently is missing in many today who claim to have curative, healing powers?

8. This is a good time in this study for a review. Can you repeat each name you have studied (eight to this point)? Can you give the definition of each?

A REVIEW

DAY TWENTY-SIX

In my walk with God, I long to develop a spiritual disposition that causes me to seek Him immediately in every situation of life. Often I simply react to a situation rather than remember how my God would have me respond because of who He is and because of what He has said.

The children of Israel were like this, too! They reacted over and over again to the circumstances of life rather than responding to the knowledge of God.

In 1 Corinthians 15, the resurrection chapter, verse

46 reads, "However, the spiritual is not first, but the natural; then the spiritual." The primary subject in 1 Corinthians 15 is the first and last Adam: our body through the first Adam is a natural body, and through the last Adam, Christ, it's a spiritual body. Within this statement is a principle—even in our reactions the natural will precede the spiritual. In other words, because we live in a natural body we can expect the natural impulse of the flesh to be first in our reactions!

Yet, if we are a new creation in Christ Jesus, we can't do whatever we want (Galatians 5:17); instead, we must "walk by the Spirit" (Galatians 5:16). To walk by the Spirit means to be controlled even in our emotional responses. To me it is simply another way of saying "be filled with the Spirit," (Ephesians 5:18). According to Galatians 5:22-23, if I am filled with the Spirit, the fruit of love, joy, peace, patience, kindness, goodness, faithfulness, gentleness, and self-control will be seen in my walk. Not one will be missing.

Now granted, the children of Israel were not indwelt by God's Spirit as we are—they had not yet entered into the New Covenant (Jeremiah 31:31-34; Ezekiel 36:26-27). However, they did know their God. They had seen His works with their own eyes. By this time in their journeys, He had made Himself known as Jehovah. He had remembered His covenant (Exodus 6:2-6) and brought them "out from under the burdens of the Egyptians" redeeming them "with an out-stretched arm and with great judgments" (Exodus 6:6). As Jehovah-jireh, He had provided their redemption from Egypt through the blood of the Passover Lamb, which was a picture of Jesus Christ (1 Corinthians 5:7). He had drowned their enemies in the Red Sea and they had sung Jehovah's praises, for they knew it was Jehovah who had delivered them.

Yet, immediately after this great victory, they reacted instead of remembering and responding to the God whose name they knew. They grumbled at the bitter waters of Marah. And it was there that in His grace and because of His lovingkindness God gave them a further revelation of what He is. He is Jehovah-rapha!

As they came to the wilderness of Sin, between Elim and Sinai, they again reacted instead of responding and calling upon their Jehovah-jireh. They were hungry, but instead of looking to the God who would provide all their needs, instead of rehearsing His past faithfulness and ways of providing, they cried, "Would that we had died by the LORD's hand in the land of Egypt, when we sat by the pots of meat, when we ate bread to the full; for you have brought us out into this wilderness to kill this whole assembly with hunger" (Exodus 16:3). Once again, God proved Himself as their Jehovah-jireh as He rained down manna from heaven. And not only manna but quails. This is the God who is able to do exceeding abundantly beyond all that we could ask or think (Ephesians 3:20).

When you read about the children of Israel, do you sometimes wonder how they could be so slow to learn? After having seen all those acts of God with their very own eyes, how could they ever murmur or complain? How could they ever doubt His protection and provision? How could they keep on reacting to these circumstances of life in such an unbelieving way rather than responding in faith and resting in the knowledge of all that they knew about God?

Do you wonder? I do! But then I look at the church, and I wonder the same thing. Oh, we haven't seen what they saw, but then they never read all that we have read in the Bible. They saw His Shekinah glory in the cloud and knew He was with them. But we have His Spirit indwelling us, bearing witness with our spirit that we are children of God and joint heirs with Christ (Romans 8:16-17). Also, we have the promise "for He Himself has said, 'I WILL NEVER DESERT YOU, NOR WILL I EVER FORSAKE YOU,' so that we confidently say, 'THE LORD IS MY HELPER, I WILL NOT BE AFRAID. WHAT

SHALL MAN DO TO ME?' " (Hebrews 13:5-6).

It is one thing to know about God and another to live in the light of that knowledge. How I pray this will not be just another study for you and me—something to store in a warehouse of knowledge rather than live. How I pray we will learn to turn to Him immediately, not reacting to the natural, but responding to the spiritual. Remember "the name of the LORD is a strong tower; the righteous runs into it and is safe" (Proverbs 18:10).

So that you will remember and call upon them in the time of need, write out the definition for each of the names of God below.

1. Elohim:

2. El Elyon:

3. El Roi:

4. El Shaddai:

5. Adonai:

6. Jehovah:

7. Jehovah-jireh:

8. Jehovah-rapha:

Day Twenty-Seven

Turn to Exodus 17 in your Bible or to the end of this day's reading (you will find the chapter there). Read it carefully, remembering all that we shared yesterday, and then follow the instructions below.

I would like to introduce you to how we do an "observation worksheet" in our Precept Upon Precept inductive Bible study courses. It is the most valuable step in inductive study. Observation is discovering what the text says; interpretation is discovering what it means; and application is then putting what you learn into practice. Let me show you how to observe the contents of this chapter step by step.

1. *Theme of Chapter, Key Words.* When you observe any chapter of a book of the Bible, you need to look for the theme of that particular passage. The theme, of course, is the main subject that the author is covering within a given text; it is what he talks about the most. In order to discover the theme of a passage, look for key words. A key word is a word that is important to the understanding of the text.

2. *Marking Key Words.* When you do an observation worksheet, you want to mark the key words of the text. This can be done one of two ways:

a. First, through the use of symbols such as

113

b. Or, by using a certain color for each key word. For example, God might be colored yellow, Israel colored red, and so on.

Every key word will have its own· individual symbol or color so that when you look at the text you can spot its usage immediately. When looking for key words, sometimes the tendency is to mark too many words. Remember, look for those words that relate to the theme of the text. Sometimes a key word may not be repeated frequently; however, you know it is key, for without it you do not know what the author is talking about.

Read through Exodus 17 and mark the words you think are the key words in this chapter. When you finish, proceed to number three.

3. *The five W's and an H.* As you read God's Word, train yourself to search out the five W's and an H.

a. *Who* wrote it or spoke it? To whom was he speaking? About whom was he speaking?

b. *What* are the main events in this chapter? The major doctrines?

c. *When* was it written or said? When did it occur?

d. *Where* did (or will) this take place? Where was it said in the Old Testament?

e. *Why* did this happen? Why was this mentioned? Why was this passed over or not acted upon?

f. *How* am I to do it? How was it done, or illustrated? How was it conveyed? How will it happen?

The answers to these five W's and an H do not need to be recorded unless you feel it is important. If you do record many of them, it is probably best to do it at the end of the observation worksheet.

4. *Contrasts, Comparisons, Terms of Conclusion, Expressions of Time.* When you read, you also want to look for:

a. *Contrasts:* a contrast is the comparison of two words to set off their dissimilar qualities. For example, light/dark, peace/contention.

b. *Words of comparison:* such as like, as, as it were.

c. *Terms of conclusion:* such as wherefore, therefore, finally.

d. *Expressions of time:* such as then, after this, until, when.

When you see any of these terms, it is good to mark them or note them in some way on your observation worksheet. For example, we use a clock to note expressions of time. We write contrasts close to the text where they appear in the right-hand margin. The left-hand margin is reserved for the paragraph divisions and titles. No other notations are made in the left-hand margin.

Read through Exodus 17 and note or mark any contrasts, terms of comparison and conclusion, and expressions of time.

I pray you are being diligent in your study. Oh, if only there were some way I could convince you of how vital all this is. Someday you are going to see Him face to face and give an account (2 Corinthians 5:10; Romans 14:10). I pray you will not be ashamed.

Observation Worksheet
EXODUS
Chapter Seventeen

Chapter Title _____

Key Verse_____

1 Then all the congregation of the sons of Israel journeyed by stages from the wilderness of Sin, according to the command of the LORD, and

camped at Rephidim, and there was no water for the people to drink.

2 Therefore the people quarreled with Moses and said, "Give us water that we may drink." And Moses said to them, "Why do you quarrel with me? Why do you test the LORD?"

3 But the people thirsted there for water; and they grumbled against Moses and said, "Why, now, have you brought us up from Egypt, to kill us and our children and our livestock with thirst?"

4 So Moses cried out to the LORD, saying, "What shall I do to this people? A little more and they will stone me."

5 Then the LORD said to Moses, "Pass before the people and take with you some of the elders of Israel; and take in your hand your staff with which you struck the Nile, and go.

6 "Behold, I will stand before you there on the rock at Horeb; and you shall strike the rock, and water will come out of it, that the people may drink." And Moses did so in the sight of the elders of Israel.

7 And he named the place Massah and Meribah because of the quarrel of the sons of Israel, and because they tested the LORD, saying, "Is the LORD among us, or not?"

8 Then Amalek came and fought against Israel at Rephidim.

9 So Moses said to Joshua, "Choose men for us, and go out, fight against Amalek. Tomorrow I will station myself on the top of the hill with the staff of God in my hand."

10 And Joshua did as Moses told him, and fought against Amalek; and Moses, Aaron, and Hur went up to the top of the hill.

11 So it came about when Moses held his hand up, that Israel prevailed, and when he let his hand down, Amalek prevailed.

12 But Moses' hands were heavy. Then they took a stone and put it under him, and he sat on it; and Aaron and Hur supported his hands, one on one side and one on the other. Thus his hands were steady until the sun set.

13 So Joshua overwhelmed Amalek and his people with the edge of the sword.

14 Then the LORD said to Moses, "Write this in a book as a memorial, and recite it to Joshua, that I will utterly blot out the memory of Amalek from under heaven."

15 And Moses built an altar, and named it The LORD is My Banner;

16 and he said, "The LORD has sworn; the LORD will have war against Amalek from generation to generation."

DAY TWENTY-EIGHT

Today we are going to continue observing Exodus 17 and tomorrow we will discuss another name of our God, Jehovah-nissi, the Lord is my Banner.

Let's move on to step five.

5. *Lists.*[1] For today, make a list of all that you learn from the text about the following:

   a. the rock
   b. Moses
   c. Amalek

Before you begin, I will give you an example and a few instructions. Make your list on scrap paper, and then, when you have it like you want it, transfer it to the right-hand margin of the observation worksheet found in yesterday's assignment. Make your list as concise as possible; don't be wordy. Record only pertinent points: significant things you learn about people, places, things, or topics in the text. Let me start you on a list about the rock—you can finish it:

The Rock
1. at Horeb
2. struck by Moses
3. _____

Don't panic. Give it a try. You are learning, so don't feel you can't do this because you haven't had training. Remember, this is between you and God. You have the Holy Spirit if you are God's child, and He is the One who reveals truth regardless of education (1 Corinthians 2:6-16).

6. *Paragraph Divisions.* Usually a chapter of the Bible will be divided into paragraphs. A paragraph contains one central thought. Paragraphs, then, are thought divisions that contribute to the whole theme of the chapter. For the purpose of study, it is good to break down a chapter into paragraphs. Then you can observe the flow of thought as the author develops his subject.

Often, paragraph divisions are already noted in your Bible. They are marked in one of three ways: either by a paragraph symbol (¶), by printing the first letter of the first word of the paragraph in bold type, or by printing the initial verse number in bold type. However, since you know what constitutes a paragraph, you can divide a chapter into paragraphs yourself.

Remember, there is nothing sacred about verse divisions, paragraph divisions, or chapter divisions. These were not noted in the original manuscripts of the Bible, but were made much later for the sake of reference.

Divide Exodus 17 into two paragraphs. Do so by drawing a line across the page between the verses where you feel the division should be.

7. *Titling Chapters and Paragraphs.* Before you title a chapter, pick out one key verse that best describes or expresses the main theme of that chapter.

In Exodus 17 that is a little difficult because of the two different events. However, for the sake of practice, do the best you can. When you choose a key verse, record it at the top of your observation worksheet.

After you choose your key verse, you are ready to title your chapter. Usually, the key verse will help you title the chapter. Your title should meet the following qualifications:

a. It should be four words or less.
b. It must contain at least one key word from the text.
c. It must be descriptive of the chapter's theme.
d. It must be distinctive from other chapter and/or paragraph titles.

Work with your title on scrap paper until you get it just like you want it, and then write it at the top of your observation worksheet.

Title your paragraphs according to the same rules for titling chapters. Each title will be written in the left-hand margin of your observation worksheet, opposite the paragraph it represents. The left margin is reserved for these titles. When you title, try to make your paragraph titles flow as grammatically and logically as possible with your chapter title.

Well, Beloved, you are finished with your observation worksheet. Let me commend you for your perseverance.

Before you finish for today, let me ask you several questions about the text. Write out your answers after each question.

1. What should have been the response of the children of Israel in their "no water" situation? Why?

2. What did smiting the rock represent? (See 1 Corinthians 10:4; John 7:37-39.)

A Review

3. What name of God would apply here? Why?

4. How can you apply this "no water" situation to your own life?

1. There are several different types of lists that we have you look for when you do Precept; however, we will leave those until you get into a regular Precept course.

THE
LORD
MY BANNER

DAY TWENTY-NINE

Exodus 17:8 states, "Then Amalek came and fought against Israel." There was to be no white flag of surrender in this battle. God was very clear, "Fight against Amalek" (v. 9). Why? Because Amalek was an enemy of God and had to be subdued, even if it meant war. Exodus 17:16 says, "The LORD has sworn; the LORD will have war against Amalek from generation to generation."

In this battle against Amalek God was first worshiped as our Jehovah-nissi, "The LORD is My Banner"

(Exodus 17:15). What is God telling us through this event? God is showing us a great principle in the Old Testament for attaining victory over our enemy, the flesh. Let me show you what I mean, step by step. Follow me carefully, give yourself time for meditation, and have a teachable spirit. Note I said "teachable" not gullible! As you go through this study, remember, "For whatever was written in earlier times was written for our instruction, that through perseverance and the encouragement of the Scriptures we might have hope" (Romans 15:4).

First of all, I believe, as do other scholars, that Amalek is a type of the flesh. A *type* is an Old Testament foreshadowing of a New Testament truth. The word *type* comes from a Greek word *tupos*. A *tupos* was a mark formed by a blow or impression with the result being a figure or an image. Romans 5:14 (KJV) says, "Nevertheless death reigned from Adam to Moses, even over them that had not sinned after the similitude of Adam's transgression, who is the figure of him that was to come." The word translated figure is the Greek word *tupos*. For example, Adam was a figure or type of Christ who was to come. In 1 Corinthians 15:45, Christ is referred to as "the last Adam."

And so we see that a type is an Old Testament shadow of a New Testament spiritual reality. A word of caution, Beloved. Typology is an exciting study that can easily get out of hand if we let our imagination rule us and are not careful to allow Scripture to interpret Scripture. (T. Norton Sterrett's book, *How to Understand Your Bible,* InterVarsity Press, has an excellent chapter on types.)

A beautiful example of a type is given to us in John 3:14-15 where Jesus likens His death on the cross to Moses lifting up the serpent in the wilderness (Numbers 21). The children of Israel had sinned and, as a result, had died from the poisonous bites of fiery serpents sent by God as just punishment. The people confessed, Moses interceded, and God commanded Moses to "make a fiery serpent, and set it on a standard; and it shall come about, that everyone who is bitten, when he looks at it, he shall live" (Numbers 21:8). Jesus, in John 3, shows that this Old Testament historical event was a foreshadow of His death on the cross; as men were saved from physical death by looking to the brass serpent on the pole, so men would be saved from spiritual death by believing in Him who was made sin for you and hung on a tree. The act of faith, looking unto Christ to save you from your death as a sinner, gives you eternal life.

Another type is found in Exodus 17, which you read yesterday. The smiting of the rock can be compared with the death of Jesus Christ, the Rock smitten for us. Remember 1 Corinthians 10:4, "And all drank the same spiritual drink, for they were drinking from a spiritual rock which followed them; and the rock was Christ." John 7:37-39 tells us that those who are thirsty are only satisfied by the water of life. "But this He spoke of the Spirit, whom those who believed in Him were to receive; for the Spirit was not yet given, because Jesus was not yet glorified" (John 7:39). The Spirit could not be given and our thirst could not be satisfied until Jesus went away. Then the Spirit came to dwell within us, sealing us until the day of our redemption. Therefore, the smitten rock and satisfying water in Exodus 17 are pictures of Jesus, God in flesh, dying for us and with that death obtaining all we need for life! (See John 16:7; 14:17; Ephesians 1:13-14.)

One of the names for God in the Old Testament, according to *The International Standard Bible Encyclopedia*, is *Zur* (or Cur, Tsur), which means *rock*. "The Rock! His work is perfect, for all His ways are just; a God of faithfulness and without injustice, righteous and upright is He. . . . You neglected the Rock who begot you, and forgot the God who gave you birth" (Deuteronomy 32:4,18).

Let's return now to our study of Jehovah-nissi, The Lord is My Banner. A banner was an ensign or standard "carried at the head of a military band or body, to indicate the line of march, or the rallying point," according to *The International Standard Bible Encyclopedia*. Nathan Stone adds: "A banner, in ancient times, was not necessarily a flag such as we use nowadays. Often it was a bare pole with a bright shining ornament which glittered in the sun."

Tomorrow I am going to share with you more about Amalek. But first, suppose I am correct in saying that Amalek is a type of the flesh and that God has a practical lesson for our lives in this historical event. Taking the story from Exodus 17 and all that you have learned these past few days, what do you think the lesson is? Meditate on it, then write out your insights below. Don't stretch your imagination or add to what God is saying; just consider all the facts (for example, what happened on the top of the hill while Joshua fought Amalek?). See what you can at this point, record it, and we will study more tomorrow. God bless you, diligent student.

DAY THIRTY

I want to give you some history of the Amalekites so that you can see how they typify our battle with the flesh, and what happens when we don't hold up our ensign or standard. I pray that as you do this study, God will minister to you, transforming you through the renewing of your mind that you might prove that gooo and acceptable and perfect will of God (Romans 12:2)

Where did Amalek come from? Remember Abraham, Isaac, and Jacob, the fathers of Israel to whom God appeared as God Almighty (El Shaddai)—the ones with whom He established His covenant forever (Exodus 6:3-4)? Well, as you probably know, Isaac had two sons, Esau and Jacob. Esau was the first-born of the twins and should have been the rightful heir to Isaac. However, Esau despised his birthright, selling it for a bowl of pottage (stew) because of the hunger of his flesh (Genesis 25:27-34; Hebrews 12:16-17). In other words, Esau's craving was so great that he sold what had eternal value in order to gain temporal satisfaction. Esau had a son and that son, Eliphaz, was the father of Amalek. Amalek then was Esau's grandson, a direct descendant of Isaac.

Amalek was also the first and constant enemy of Israel. Numbers 24:20 says, "And he [Balaam, son of Beor] looked at Amalek and took up his discourse and said, 'Amalek was the first of the nations, but his end shall be destruction.' " By "the first of the nations," Balaam was saying that Amalek was the first of the nations to trouble Israel. How true this was! After the children of Israel had come out of Egypt through the Passover and crossed the Red Sea by the mighty salvation of the Lord (Exodus 14:13), and after they had eaten bread from heaven and had drunk water from the rock, the first enemy they had to deal with was Amalek (Exodus 17:8).

Isn't the flesh your first and constant enemy also? Later, Moses would write, "Remember what Amalek did to you along the way when you came out from Egypt, how he met you along the way and attacked among you all the stragglers at your rear when you were faint and weary; and he did not fear God. Therefore it shall come about when the LORD your God has given you rest from all your surrounding enemies, in the land which the LORD your God gives you as an inheritance to possess, you shall blot out the memory of Amalek from under heaven; you must not forget" (Deuteronomy 25:17-19). Note the phrase, "He did not fear God." The word fear means to reverence, to respect, or to honor God as God. Just as Esau despised his birthright, not giving it proper value or respect, so his grandson Amalek did not respect God. Esau's birthright would have made him an heir to the Abrahamic covenant, yet he sold it because of temporal, fleshly hunger!

O Beloved, can you see the parallels to our flesh? Like Esau, the flesh cannot wait; its cravings must be satisfied now. Not later, but now! Like Amalek, the flesh knows no respect or reverence for God or for the things of God; rather, the deeds of the flesh are "immorality, impurity, sensuality, idolatry, sorcery, enmities, strife, jealousy, outbursts of anger, disputes, dissensions, factions, envying, drunkenness, carousing" (Galatians 5:19-21). All of those things belong to Egypt, the world, not to the redeemed child of God brought out of slavery, out of the land of bondage. "Whosoever committeth sin is the servant of sin" (John 8:34, KJV), but "if the Son, therefore, shall make you free, ye shall be free indeed" (John 8:36, KJV).

What is the greatest enemy of the child of God? What is the first enemy a Christian has to deal with after he is saved? Who attacks you from your rear when you are faint and weary (Deuteronomy 25:18)? Is it not your flesh? Is this not why Paul, who couldn't wait to get rid of this mortal body, groaned, "longing to be clothed with our dwelling from heaven" (2 Corinthians 5:2)? A perpetual warfare is waging in our bodies: "For the flesh sets its desire against the Spirit and the Spirit against the flesh; for these are in opposition to one another, so that you may not do the things that you please" (Galatians 5:17). We can't do the things we please; rather, we must constantly be on the alert, ever cognizant of the promise that if we walk by the Spirit we "will not carry out the desire of the flesh" (Galatians 5:16).

The flesh must constantly be put to death. It can't be tolerated, catered to, or spared in any way. If it is, it will devastate you. God gives us a very clear picture of this in the story of King Saul.

1 SAMUEL 15:1-3

Then Samuel said to Saul, "The LORD sent me to anoint you as king over His people, over Israel; now therefore, listen to the words of the LORD. Thus says the LORD of hosts, 'I will punish Amalek *for* what he did to Israel, how he set himself against him on the way while he was coming up from Egypt. Now go and strike Amalek and utterly destroy all that he has, and do not spare him; but put to death both man and woman, child and infant, ox and sheep, camel and donkey.' "

1 SAMUEL 15:7-9

So Saul defeated the Amalekites, from Havilah as you go to Shur, which is east of Egypt. And he captured Agag the king of the Amalekites alive, and utterly destroyed all the people with the edge of the sword. But Saul and the people spared Agag and the best of the sheep, the oxen, the fatlings, the lambs, and all that was good, and were not willing to destroy them utterly; but everything despised and worthless, that they utterly destroyed.

And how did God, the Lord of hosts, feel about Saul's incomplete obedience? "Then the word of the LORD came to Samuel, saying, 'I regret that I have made Saul king, for he has turned back from following Me, and has not carried out My commands' " (1 Samuel 15:10-11).

God was distressed and so was Samuel, the prophet, when he confronted Saul. And how did Saul respond? Did he have a godly sorrow that led to repentance? Read on.

1 Samuel 15:16-23

Then Samuel said to Saul, "Wait, and let me tell you what the LORD said to me last night." And he said to him, "Speak!" And Samuel said, "Is it not true, though you were little in your own eyes, you were *made* the head of the tribes of Israel? And the LORD anointed you king over Israel, and the LORD sent you on a mission, and said, 'Go and utterly destroy the sinners, the Amalekites, and fight against them until they are exterminated.' Why then did you not obey the voice of the LORD, but rushed upon the spoil and did what was evil in the sight of the LORD?" Then Saul said to Samuel, "I did obey the voice of the LORD, and went on the mission on which the LORD sent me, and have brought back Agag the king of Amalek, and have utterly destroyed the Amalekites. But the people took *some* of the spoil, sheep and oxen, the choicest of the things devoted to destruction, to sacrifice to the LORD your God at Gilgal." And Samuel said, "Has the LORD as much delight in burnt offerings and sacrifices as in obeying the voice of the LORD? Behold, to obey is better than sacrifice, *and* to heed than the fat of rams. For rebellion is as the sin of divination, and insubordination is as iniquity and idolatry. Because you have rejected the word of the LORD, He has also rejected you from *being* king."

I want you to have time to think about all you are reading, Beloved. These are lessons that can make the difference between victory and defeat, between being used of God or being a castaway (1 Corinthians 9:24-27), between a full life of service to God or possibly a premature death as God's judgment upon sin, leaving the Christian ashamed before God (1 Corinthians 11:28-32; Ecclesiastes 7:17; Hebrews 12:9; 1 Corinthians 5:5; 1 John 5:16).

Therefore, from the scriptures you have read in 1 Samuel 15, answer the questions that follow. Meditate on all that has been said, and then we will wrap it up tomorrow.

1. List exactly what the Lord of hosts told Saul to do.

2. What did Saul spare and why?

3. How did Saul respond when confronted with his disobedience?

4. What did Saul lose because of his disobedience?

5. What can you learn from all this for your own life?

Day Thirty-One

Yesterday I said that the flesh could not be tolerated, catered to, or spared in any way. The flesh must be put to death; otherwise it will devastate you. Paul says in Galatians 5:24, "Now those who belong to Christ Jesus have crucified the flesh with its passions and desires."

This is depicted in the life of King Saul. God told Saul through Samuel the prophet to "strike Amalek and utterly destroy all that he has, and do not spare him; but put to death both man and woman, child and infant, ox and sheep, camel and donkey" (1 Samuel 15:3). Not one vestige of the Amalekites was to be spared and Saul was to do the killing. It is the same in Galatians 5:24. The verb "have crucified" is an aorist active indicative verb; therefore, it is the Christian's responsibility to do the crucifying! Aorist tense indicates that the action is performed at one particular point in time. The indicative mood is the mood of reality, of certainty. Death to the flesh is to be the battle cry of every child of God.

"But how?" you ask. And "Why?" Because if you do not declare the flesh, with its passions and lusts, dead, it can kill you. This is exactly what happened to Saul. He did not fully obey God. Instead of destroying every last Amalekite and their possessions, he saved the best to sacrifice to God (1 Samuel 15:15). Instead of destroying Agag, king of the Amalekites, he brought him back captive, only to become the captive of an Amalekite eventually and die by his hand. In 2 Samuel 1:6-10, you can read about the Amalekite who dealt Saul his final death blow, and in so doing, removed the crown from his head.

O Beloved, this is what I see, what I read of, what I hear about, happening all over Christendom these days. Crowns being snatched from the heads of Christians because the flesh was not crucified—constantly reckoned dead. Christian leaders, authors, pastors, workers, and people in the pews have lost their crowns because they have spared an Amalekite and its possessions, thinking that there was some good there that could be used as a sacrifice for Christ. When will we agree with God and say, "For I know that nothing good dwells in me, that is, in my flesh" (Romans 7:18)? When will we determine that we will walk by the Spirit who dwells within every believer? When will we acknowledge that there is a war to be fought?

When Israel came out of Egypt and crossed the Red Sea with the Egyptians pursuing, Moses said, "Stand still, and see the salvation of the LORD" (Exodus 14:13, KJV). That's salvation! But when along came Amalek, it was "Go out and fight against Amalek." That's Christian warfare. We want salvation, but not warfare. When will we rally at His standard, the banner of our Jehovah-nissi? True, the battle rages between flesh and Spirit as it did between Joshua and Amalek in the valley of Rephidim. Yet, look up. There on the holy mount of heavenly Zion is the Son of God with arms extended high, ever living to make intercession for you (Hebrews 7:25). All power and authority have been given to Him, and what is His is yours. You are a joint heir with Christ (Romans 8:17). Therefore, you have no reason or excuse for waving the flag of surrender. Stand firm. "Be strong in the Lord, and in the strength of His might" (Ephesians 6:10). Fight the good fight (2 Timothy 4:7). Of course there is a battle, "but thanks be to God, who always leads us in His triumph in Christ" (2 Corinthians 2:14).

You are not alone on that battlefield; look to the Lord your banner. It is also His battle. Note the words, "The LORD will have war against Amalek from generation to generation" (Exodus 17:16). It is the Lord's battle; victory depends on His rod being lifted up. The flesh is in opposition to the Spirit, God's resident, indwelling Holy Spirit. What part do you play in it all? Are you to sit in the grandstands eating hot dogs, drinking sodas, and giving a hoot and a holler every now and then? That is where most Christians are, and that is why our "team" is losing. But you, O valiant warrior, are to put on the full armor of God and get on the battlefront. Under His banner, victory is always assured. "And he shall say to them, 'Hear, O Israel, you are approaching the battle against your enemies today. Do not be faint-hearted. Do not be afraid, or panic, or tremble before them, for the LORD your God is the one who goes with you, to fight for you against your enemies, to save

131

you' " (Deuteronomy 20:3-4).

Do you see what God is trying to show us in the battle against Amalek? When Moses' hand was up, Israel prevailed. When it came down, Amalek prevailed. And what was in Moses' hand? The rod of God. The rod which became a serpent and swallowed Pharaoh's rods which had turned into serpents. The rod that turned water into blood. The rod that brought plagues upon the land of Egypt. The rod that parted the Red Sea. The rod of Elohim,[1] the one who spoke and brought the worlds into existence, the one who created you for His glory. Elohim, the one who, by His power, is able to subdue all that He has created.

Wow! It's exciting, isn't it? I could go on and on, but you may be weary or your head may be spinning. If so, reread this until every fiber of your being absorbs the blessed reality of it all. Under the banner of God, victory is always assured; but apart from it, defeat is a certainty. When the banner of God's rod was not held high, Amalek prevailed. You can't do battle against the flesh under your own power. This truth is so clearly illustrated for us in Numbers 14:40-45. Let me give you the setting of this passage. Remember when the twelve spies from the children of Israel spied out Canaan and ten brought back an evil report?

NUMBERS 13:32-14:4

"The land through which we have gone, in spying it out, is a land that devours its inhabitants; and all the people whom we saw in it are men of *great* size. There also we saw the Nephilim (the sons of Anak are part of the Nephilim); and we became like grasshoppers in our own sight, and so we were in their sight." Then all the congregation lifted up their voices and cried, and the people wept that night. And all the sons of Israel grumbled against Moses and Aaron; and the whole congregation said to them, "Would that we had died in the land of Egypt! Or would that we had died in the wilderness! And why is the LORD bringing us into this land, to fall by the sword? Our wives and our little ones will become plunder; would it not be better for us to return to Egypt?" So they said to one another, "Let us appoint a leader and return to Egypt."

When Moses pointed out to them the sin of their unbelief and told them the consequences, forty years of wandering and dying in the wilderness, they then decided they would go on into Canaan.

NUMBERS 14:40-45

In the morning, however, they rose up early and went up to the ridge of the hill country, saying, "Here we are; we have indeed sinned, but we will go up to the place which the LORD has promised." But Moses said, "Why then are you transgressing the commandment of the LORD, when it will not succeed? Do not go up, lest you be struck down before your enemies, for the LORD is not among you. For the Amalekites and the Canaanites will be there in front of you, and you will fall by the sword, inasmuch as you have turned back from following the LORD. And the LORD will not be with you." But they went up heedlessly to the ridge of the hill country; neither the ark of the covenant of the LORD nor Moses left the camp. Then the Amalekites and the Canaanites who lived in that hill country came down, and struck them and beat them down as far as Hormah.

In this instance, the children of Israel were defeated by the Amalekites because the Lord did not go with them. O Beloved, if you don't learn anything else, learn this: Apart from Him you can do nothing (John

15:5). Only by abiding under the power, the standard, the banner, the ensign of your Jehovah-nissi can you have victory over the flesh, the world, and the devil, your enemies and God's.

I long to see the church awakened and prepared for battle. I fear for the stragglers at the rear who are faint and weary (Deuteronomy 25:18), entangled with the affairs of this life (2 Timothy 2:4), and vulnerable prey to the attack of Amalek. Remember, that which Saul spared slayed him. God is no respecter of persons; the same thing will happen to you if you don't destroy Amalek and all that belongs to him! Excuses won't do. You can't blame others as Saul did. It is your crown that will fall from your head. What do you need to put to death? Go to war and know that Christ is there with you, interceding on heavenly Zion's holy mount. Victory is forthcoming. "Now to Him who is able to do exceeding abundantly beyond all that we ask or think, according to the power that works within us, to Him be the glory in the church and in Christ Jesus to all generations forever and ever. Amen." (Ephesians 3:20-21).

Note

1. The rod of God, or staff of God, in Exodus 17:9 is the rod of Elohim in the Hebrew.

DISCUSSION QUESTIONS FOR DAYS 26 THROUGH 31

1. Explain what Jehovah-nissi means.

2. In Exodus 17, we see the children of Israel in two different situations. What are the situations?

3. What was the attitude of the Israelites in the "no water" situation?

4. Why do you think they had this attitude?

5. Assuming that Amalek is a type of the flesh, what characteristics did you glean from your study that would be descriptive of the flesh?

6. What strategy do you see in Exodus 17 for dealing with the flesh?

7. What was the role of Jehovah-nissi in the battle?

8. From your study, what do you see as the Christian's responsibility in dealing with the flesh? Why?

9. What was Saul's fatal mistake in his dealings with Agag?

10. In examining your own life, how have you dealt with your flesh?

    a. Have you dealt with the flesh in your own power? What was the result?

    b. Have you dealt with the flesh under the banner of Jehovah-nissi? What was the result?

THE LORD WHO SANCTIFIES YOU

DAY THIRTY-TWO

You can study for a life-time and yet never mine all the precious gems of truth hidden in God's Word. How can we sell our souls for tinsel when silver could be ours? How can we wear the clothes of spiritual paupers when the coffers of the King of kings are ours for the claiming? O church, church, why have you asked for your inheritance, taken it to a far country, squandered it on the fleeting pleasure of this world, and found yourself eating the husks from the pig's trough when you could be dining at the King's table?

The Lord Sanctifies You

Am I speaking to you? You can tell by what is foremost in your life, by what you give yourself to! How important is God's Word? How devoted are you to really learning it so that you can live by every word that proceeds out of the mouth of God (Deuteronomy 8:3)? Are you spoon-fed, or are you learning to feed yourself? Do you flirt with Christianity, or do you love God with *all* your heart, *all* your mind, *all* your strength?

The name of God that was next revealed to the children of Israel is Jehovah-mekoddishkem (also spelled mekaddishkem), the Lord sanctifies you.

When the children of Israel "set out from Rephidim, they came to the wilderness of Sinai, and camped in the wilderness; and there Israel camped in front of the mountain. And Moses went up to God, and the Lord called to him from the mountain, saying, 'Thus you shall say to the house of Jacob and tell the sons of Israel: "You yourselves have seen what I did to the Egyptians, and *how* I bore you on eagles' wings, and brought you to Myself. Now then, if you will indeed obey My voice and keep My covenant, then you shall be My own possession among all the peoples, for all the earth is Mine; and you shall be to Me a kingdom of priests and a holy nation"'" (Exodus 19:2-6).

Israel was to be, as we are, a kingdom of priests and a holy nation (1 Peter 2:9). Thus, God brought His people to Mount Sinai where He gave them the covenant of the Law and the pattern of the tabernacle where they would worship their God. These commandments would set them apart as a peculiar people for God's own possession. Here they would come to know Jehovah as Jehovah-mekoddishkem through observing His sabbaths.

EXODUS 31:12-18
And the Lord spoke to Moses, saying, "But as for you, speak to the sons of Israel, saying,

'You shall surely observe My sabbaths; for *this* is a sign between Me and you throughout your generations, that you may know that I am the LORD who sanctifies you. Therefore you are to observe the sabbath, for it is holy to you. Everyone who profanes it shall surely be put to death; for whoever does any work on it, that person shall be cut off from among his people. For six days work may be done, but on the seventh day there is a sabbath of complete rest, holy to the LORD; whoever does any work on the sabbath day shall surely be put to death. So the sons of Israel shall observe the sabbath, to celebrate the sabbath throughout their generations as a perpetual covenant. It is a sign between Me and the sons of Israel forever; for in six days the LORD made heaven and earth, but on the seventh day He ceased *from labor,* and was refreshed.' " And when He had finished speaking with him upon Mount Sinai, He gave Moses the two tablets of the testimony, tablets of stone, written by the finger of God.

The words *sanctify, set apart, holy,* and *saint* come from the common root words *qadash* in the Hebrew and *hagios* in the Greek. For the first time in the Word of God, the purpose of and the command for the Sabbath is laid down before the children if Israel. The Sabbath is to be a sign between God and Israel throughout all their generations. The purpose of the Sabbath was, "That you may know that I am the LORD who sanctifies you" (Exodus 31:13) or "That you may know that I am Jehovah-mekoddishkem." As God made the Sabbath holy to the children of Israel, so He made the children of Israel holy, or set apart, unto Himself.

What is the purpose of our redemption? To make us righteous, to make us holy. Only holiness can abide in the presence of the Most Holy God. Therefore, God tells us in Hebrews 12:14 (KJV), "Follow . . . holiness, without which no man shall see the Lord." Holiness is not an option, it's a requirement! The constant observance of the sabbath, week in and week out, was to remind the children of Israel that they were "A CHOSEN RACE, A ROYAL PRIESTHOOD, A HOLY NATION, A PEOPLE FOR *God's* OWN POSSESSION" (1 Peter 2:9). The gravity of their sanctification was seen in the punishment due those who broke the Sabbath.

EXODUS 31:14-15

Therefore you are to observe the sabbath, for it is holy to you. Everyone who profanes it shall surely be put to death; for whoever does any work on it, that person shall be cut off from among his people. For six days work may be done, but on the seventh day there is a sabbath of complete rest, holy to the LORD; whoever does any work on the sabbath day shall surely be put to death.

As I said before, holiness was not an option. It was part of "A perpetual covenant . . . a sign between Me and the sons of Israel forever." As God sanctified Israel, so He sanctifies the church. And how does He sanctify us? Read the scriptures below and after each one write what that scripture says about our sanctification:

HEBREWS 10:10-14

By this will we have been sanctified through the offering of the body of Jesus Christ once for all. And every priest stands daily ministering and offering time after time the same sacrifices, which can never take away sins; but He, having offered one sacrifice for sins for all time, SAT DOWN AT THE RIGHT HAND OF GOD, waiting from that time onward UNTIL HIS ENEMIES BE MADE

A FOOTSTOOL FOR HIS FEET. For by one offering
He has perfected for all time those who are
sanctified.

JOHN 17:15-19

"I do not ask Thee to take them out of the
world, but to keep them from the evil *one*.
They are not of the world, even as I am not of
the world. Sanctify them in the truth; Thy word
is truth. As Thou didst send Me into the world,
I also have sent them into the world. And for
their sakes I sanctify Myself, that they themselves also may be sanctified in truth."

1 THESSALONIANS 4:3-8

For this is the will of God, your sanctification;
that is, that you abstain from sexual immorality;
that each of you know how to possess his own
vessel in sanctification and honor, not in lustful
passion, like the Gentiles who do not know
God; *and* that no man transgress and defraud
his brother in the matter because the Lord is
the avenger in all these things, just as we also
told you before and solemnly warned *you*. For
God has not called us for the purpose of impurity, but in sanctification. Consequently, he
who rejects *this* is not rejecting man but the
God who gives His Holy Spirit to you.

1 Thessalonians 5:23

Now may the God of peace Himself sanctify you entirely; and may your spirit and soul and body be preserved complete, without blame at the coming of our Lord Jesus Christ.

Ephesians 5:25-27

Husbands, love your wives, just as Christ also loved the church and gave Himself up for her; that He might sanctify her, having cleansed her by the washing of water with the word, that He might present to Himself the church in all her glory, having no spot or wrinkle or any such thing; but that she should be holy and blameless.

2 Peter 1:4

For by these He has granted to us His precious and magnificent promises, in order that by them you might become partakers of *the* divine nature, having escaped the corruption that is in the world by lust.

Now, look at Leviticus 20:7-8. I have a few comments, and then some questions for you.

LEVITICUS 20:7-8

"You shall consecrate yourselves therefore and be holy, for I am the LORD your God. And you shall keep My statutes and practice them; I am the LORD who sanctifies you."

Here again we see His name, Jehovah-mekod-dishkem. Leviticus is the book that tells the children of Israel how to worship their God. Its theme is the sanctification of the people of God, a sanctification that affects the way they walk, the way they live, the way they worship. Redemption is not the end of us; rather, it is sanctification that prepares us for glorification. Once God's people are redeemed, as seen in Exodus, they are to move on to sanctification, as seen in Leviticus. There can be no sanctification without redemption; however, redemption always produces sanctification to one degree or another. The death of Christ provides for our redemption, for "without shedding of blood there is no forgiveness" of sins (Hebrews 9:22). The resurrection of Christ provides us with the ability to walk in newness of life through the gift of the Holy Spirit who sets us free from the law of sin and death (Romans 6:4; 8:2-4). Thus the God who sanctified Israel is the God who sanctifies the church.

Write your answers to the following questions.

1. According to the scriptures you have read today, how is the church sanctified?

2. How was Israel sanctified?

143

3. What parts of your being are to be sanctified?

4. When did your sanctification begin and who began it?

5. How is your sanctification continued? By whom?

6. Are you actively pursuing holiness? List the specific ways you are doing this.

7. Can you really live a holy life apart from God's Word? Are you studying it? Why don't you get into Precept Upon Precept; it will transform you. (For information on our Precept Bible study courses, see the last page.)

Jehovah-mekoddishkem has said, "Thus you are to be holy to Me, for I the LORD am holy; and I have set you apart from the peoples to be Mine" (Leviticus 20:26).

What will you say to Him?

1. Define Jehovah-mekoddishkem.

2. What was the sign between God and Israel indicating that He was Jehovah-mekoddishkem? Why did it exist?

3. What was the purpose of the Sabbath for the children of Israel?

4. What did you learn about your relationship to Jehovah-mekoddishkem?

5. If the Lord is your righteousness, how does that affect your life?

6. How important is holiness in your life? (See Hebrews 12:14.)

7. Are you set apart? If so, from what? How is your life different from those who do not know Christ?

THE
LORD
IS PEACE

DAY THIRTY-THREE

In the dark hours of Israel's history God revealed Himself to Gideon as Jehovah-shalom, the Lord is peace. Gideon was a young man whose family was the least in Manasseh. Things were bad. "Israel was brought very low because of Midian" (Judges 6:6). The sons of Israel had done "what was evil in the sight of the LORD; and the LORD gave them into the hands of Midian seven years. And the power of Midian prevailed against Israel. Because of Midian the sons of Israel made for themselves the dens which were in the mountains and the caves and the strongholds. For it was when Israel had sown, that the Midianites would come up with the Amalekites and the sons of the east and go against them. So they would camp against them and destroy the produce of the earth as far as Gaza, and leave no sustenance in Israel as well as no sheep, ox, or donkey. For they would come up with their livestock and their tents, they would come in like locusts for number, both they and their camels were innumerable; and they came into the land to devastate it" (Judges 6:1-5).

When the hour is dark and the situation desperate, we finally long for God's peace. Then we crave it; our sanity depends on it. Fear grips us. Trembling, we grope through the darkness longing for peace's reassurance that all will be all right. Yet the fear that comes from the circumstances of this life is nothing compared with the fear that can come when one finds himself face to face with God Himself.

Someday we are going to stand naked, one by one, before the very person of God Himself. Christian and non-Christian will give account to Him for the way they have lived. The lost will stand at the Great White Throne (Revelation 20:11-15). The Christians will stand at the Judgment Seat of Christ: "For we must all appear before the judgment seat of Christ, that each one may be recompensed for his deeds in the body, according to what he has done, whether good or bad (2 Corinthians 5:10). "But you, why do you judge your brother? Or you again, why do you regard your brother with contempt? For we shall all stand before the judgment seat of God. For it is written, 'AS I LIVE, SAYS THE LORD, EVERY KNEE SHALL BOW TO ME, AND EVERY TONGUE SHALL GIVE PRAISE TO GOD.' So then each one of us shall give account of himself to God" (Romans 14:10-12).

Gideon wasn't afraid until he realized he had seen the angel of the Lord face to face. "When Gideon saw that he was the angel of the LORD, he said, 'Alas O Lord GOD! For now I have seen the angel of the LORD face to face.' And the LORD said to him, 'Peace to you, do not fear; you shall not die.' Then Gideon built an altar there to the LORD and named it The LORD is Peace" (Judges 6:22-24). How rightly Gideon named that altar, The Lord is Peace. True peace cannot be found in any other place than in a right relationship with God.

Take a moment to read the following scriptures and note below each what you learn about peace and its relationship to God.

LEVITICUS 26:2-6

"You shall keep My sabbaths and reverence My sanctuary; I am the LORD. If you walk in My statutes and keep My commandments so as to carry them out, then I shall give you rains in their season, so that the land will yield its produce and the trees of the field will bear their fruit. Indeed, your threshing will last for you until grape gathering, and grape gathering will last until sowing time. You will thus eat your food to the full and live securely in your land. I shall also grant peace in the land, so that you may lie down with no one making *you* tremble. I shall also eliminate harmful beasts from the land, and no sword will pass through your land."

NUMBERS 6:22-27

Then the LORD spoke to Moses, saying, "Speak to Aaron and to his sons, saying, 'Thus you shall bless the sons of Israel. You shall say to them: The LORD bless you, and keep you; the LORD make His face shine on you, and be gracious to you; the LORD lift up His countenance on you, and give you peace.' So they shall invoke My name on the sons of Israel, and I then will bless them."

JEREMIAH 29:11

"For I know the plans that I have for you," declares the LORD, "plans for welfare and not for calamity to give you a future and a hope."

Isaiah 48:18

"If only you had paid attention to My commandments! Then your well-being would have been like a river, and your righteousness like the waves of the sea."

ISAIAH 26:3

Thou wilt keep *him* in perfect peace, *whose* mind *is* stayed *on thee,* because he trusteth in thee (KJV).

PSALM 119:165

Those who love Thy law have great peace, and nothing causes them to stumble.

PHILIPPIANS 4:4-7

Rejoice in the Lord always; again I will say, rejoice! Let your forbearing *spirit* be know to all men. The Lord is near. Be anxious for nothing, but in everything by prayer and supplication with thanksgiving let your requests be made known to God. And the peace of God, which surpasses all comprehension, shall guard your hearts and your minds in Christ Jesus.

PHILIPPIANS 4:8-9

Finally, brethren, whatever is true, whatever is honorable, whatever is right, whatever is pure, whatever is lovely, whatever is of good repute, if there is any excellence and if anything worthy of praise, let your mind dwell on these things. The things you have learned and received and heard and seen in me, practice these things; and the God of peace shall be with you.

In Isaiah 9:6, God gave His people a wonderful promise: "For a child will be born to us, a son will be given to us; and the government will rest on His shoulders; and His name will be called Wonderful Counselor, Mighty God, Eternal Father, Prince of Peace." Here He is Jesus, our Jehovah-shalom, the Prince of Peace, the one who reconciles us to God, who enables us to stand before Him face to face without fear. "Therefore having been justified by faith, we have peace with God through our Lord Jesus Christ" (Romans 5:1).

He gives us a peace that does not alter, regardless of circumstances, for the peace He gives us is ever resident in the one who promised, " 'I WILL NEVER DESERT YOU, NOR WILL I EVER FORSAKE YOU,' so that we confidently say, 'THE LORD IS MY HELPER, I WILL NOT BE AFRAID. WHAT SHALL MAN DO TO ME?' " (Hebrews 13:5-6). Therefore, when others about us are fainting for fear, we can "exult in our tribulations, knowing that tribulation brings about perseverance; and perseverance, proven character; and proven character, hope; and hope does not disappoint, because the love of God has been poured out within our hearts through the Holy Spirit who was given to us" (Romans 5:3-5). "For God hath not given us the spirit of fear but of power, and of love, and of a sound mind" (2 Timothy 1:7, KJV). Thus, He says, "Peace I leave with you; My peace I give to you; not as the world gives, do I give to you. Let not your heart be troubled, nor let it be fearful" (John 14:27).

Beloved, where do you run when you need peace? Peace is only found in Jehovah-shalom. He will keep you in perfect peace when your mind is stayed upon Him (Isaiah 26:3). If peace eludes you, you are not filled by His Spirit, for the fruit of the Spirit is love, joy, peace (Galatians 5:22). So abide in Him, being filled with the Holy Spirit (Ephesians 5:18).

"Now the God of peace be with you all. Amen" (Romans 15:33).

1. What kind of peace does Jehovah-shalom bring?

2. From your study, how do you walk with Jehovah-shalom?

3. In practical terms, how do you maintain peace?

4. Are you habitually walking in peace? If not, what fear is keeping you from having His peace? Can you think of any name of God that covers that fear?

THE
LORD
OF HOSTS

DAY THIRTY-FOUR

I often think of our brothers and sisters in Christ who have lived under the iron heel of communism. What kept their Christianity from being stamped out by all the threats and atrocities that godless governments hold over their heads?

Have you read their stories and wondered how they endured? Have you wondered whether you would persevere in the face of persecution? Why do you wonder? Why do you doubt the strength of your commitment to Jesus Christ? I suspect its because you have never been in a position like theirs. It has never cost you to be a follower of Jesus Christ, so when you try to imagine how you would react, you can only look at your own weaknesses and assume that you would fail! Some of you assume that since you have difficulty witnessing now—standing for Christ in a society like ours—you would never stand in an adverse society!

My friend, if you had come to the end of your strength and needed deliverance, you might seek refuge in a place that seemed unnatural to you. You might turn to Jehovah-sabaoth, the Lord of hosts.

When there seemed to be no other recourse for deliverance, the children of Israel came to know God as Jehovah-sabaoth.

The name Jehovah-sabaoth is not used until the book of 1 Samuel, and then in two out of three instances it is used by individuals. Apparently at that time Israel did not see her need to call upon Him as Lord of hosts. Yet, when we read the prophets Isaiah, Jeremiah, Amos, Haggai, Zechariah, and Malachi, we find this name for God used over and over again. It appears fifty-two times in Zechariah's fourteen chapters and eighty-three times in Jeremiah's fifty-two chapters.

Why is God repeatedly referred to as the Lord of hosts in Isaiah and Jeremiah but not in Ezekiel? Because this name belongs to a certain stage in the experience of God's people. It is God's name for man's extremity. Not until we, as God's chosen people, find ourselves failing and powerless do we realize our need to run to our Jehovah-sabaoth. This is a name for those who, in the midst of a struggle, find their resources inadequate. It is not a name for those who have ceased to fight. Therefore, you won't find it in Ezekiel; in Ezekiel's day God's people were to settle down for seventy years of captivity. This is our name to run to when, from our perspective, there is no other help.

From God's perspective, it is a name that reminds His people of exactly who He is, the Lord of hosts. Not only the one who delivers, but also the one who judges. Thus, we see God in the book of Malachi reminding His people over and over again of His name Jehovah-sabaoth: " 'I am not pleased with you,' says the LORD of hosts . . . 'I am a great King,' says the LORD of hosts, 'and My name is feared among the nations' " (Malachi 1:10,14).

In Malachi, twenty-two of the twenty-four usages of this name appear in the phrase "saith the Lord of hosts," indicating a direct word from God. Malachi was written to a people who honored God with their lips but not with their lives; therefore, once again, we see man's failures. God wanted them to see Him as Lord of hosts and bow the knee. This is His name to meet failure and offer deliverance. O Beloved, do not forget it, for it is "a strong tower; the righteous runs into it and is safe" (Proverbs 18:10). It is a name that keeps you from boasting in chariots and horses (Psalm 20:7), for who needs them when the name of his God is the Lord of hosts!

Let's look at some usages of this name and note the circumstances surrounding them. After you read these verses, write out your insights about how Jehovah-sabaoth figures in these circumstances.

The first two instances of Jehovah-sabaoth are in 1 Samuel 1:3-11. This incident occurred in the final days of the judges. In the days of Samuel, the last judge, we find a transition in Israel's history from a theocracy to a monarchy.[1]

1 SAMUEL 1:1-3

Now there was a certain man from Ramathaim-zophim from the hill country of Ephraim, and his name was Elkanah the son of Jeroham, the son of Elihu, the son of Tohu, the son of Zuph, an Ephraimite. And he had two wives: the name of one was Hannah and the name of the other Peninnah; and Peninnah had children, but Hannah had no children. Now this man would go up from his city yearly to worship and to sacrifice to the LORD of hosts in Shiloh. And the two sons of Eli, Hophni and Phinehas were priests to the LORD there.

Because God had closed Hannah's womb, it brought her great distress from Peninnah, Elkanah's other wife.

1 SAMUEL 1:6-7, 10-11

Her rival, however, would provoke her bitterly to irritate her, because the LORD had closed her womb. And it happened year after year, as often as she went up to the house of the LORD, she would provoke her, so she wept and would not eat. . . . And she, greatly distressed, prayed to the LORD and wept bitterly. And she made a vow and said, "O LORD of hosts, if Thou wilt indeed look on the affliction of Thy maidservant, and remember me, and not forget thy maidservant, but wilt give Thy maidservant a son, then I will give him to the LORD all the days of his life, and a razor shall never come on his head.

God answered that prayer and gave Samuel to Hannah.

The fourth usage of Jehovah-sabaoth in 1 Samuel occurs as David faces the Philistine giant, Goliath. (We will look at the third usage of Jehovah-sabaoth later. At this point, I am not following a chronological order because the third usage concerns a nation rather than an individual.)

1 SAMUEL 17:42-47

When the Philistine looked and saw David, he disdained him; for he was *but* a youth, and ruddy, with a handsome appearance. And the Philistine said to David, "Am I a dog, that you come to me with sticks?" And the Philistine cursed David by his gods. The Philistine also said to David, "Come to me, and I will give your flesh to the birds of the sky and the beasts of the field." Then David said to the Philistine, "You come to me with a sword, a spear, and a javelin, but I come to you in the name of the LORD of hosts, the God of the armies of Israel, whom you have taunted. This day the LORD will deliver you up into my hands, and I will strike you down and remove your head from you. And I will give the dead bodies of the army of the Philistines this day to the birds of the sky and the wild beasts of the earth, that all the earth may know that there is a God in Israel, and that all this assembly may know that the LORD does not deliver by sword or by spear; for the battle is the LORD's and He will give you into our hands."

Insights:

Both Hannah and David called upon the Lord of hosts and found deliverance through His name. Deliverance is there for you as well—whatever your situation. Yet His name cannot be used as a sort of magic cure-all. Remember, it is the righteous who run into it and are safe (Proverbs 18:10). In the third occurrence of Jehovah-sabaoth in 1 Samuel, as it falls chronologically, we find the Israelites in conflict with the Philistines.

1 SAMUEL 4:3-4

When the people came into the camp, the elders of Israel said, "Why has the LORD defeated us today before the Philistines? Let us take to ourselves from Shiloh the ark of the covenant of the LORD, that it may come among us and deliver us from the power of our enemies." So the people sent to Shiloh, and from there they carried the ark of the covenant of the LORD of hosts who sits *above* the cherubim; and the two sons of Eli, Hophni and Phinehas, *were* there with the ark of the covenant of God.

God's people thought that all they needed was the presence of the ark of the covenant of the Lord of hosts. Certainly, then deliverance would come from Jehovah-sabaoth. But they were wrong. Religion does not deliver—only righteousness delivers.

1 SAMUEL 4:10-11

So the Philistines fought and Israel was defeated, and every man fled to his tent, and the slaughter was very great; for there fell of Israel thirty thousand foot soldiers. And the ark of God was taken; and the two sons of Eli, Hophni and Phinehas, died.

Do you see? Do you understand? His name is there as a strong tower for us to call on, but we can't misuse it. If we want deliverance, we must come to Him in righteousness.

"But," you say, "I have no righteousness." True, in

and of ourselves we have none. Yet, His righteousness is available to us, for He is Jehovah-tsidkenu, the Lord our righteousness. We will study this soon, but until then "Thus says the LORD of hosts, 'Consider your ways!' " (Haggai 1:7).

Could you endure if you had to physically suffer for your faith? Of course, for the name of your God is the Lord of hosts . . . "the righteous runs into it and is safe" (Proverbs 18:10).

JEREMIAH 20:11-13

But the LORD is with me like a dread champion; therefore my persecutors will stumble and not prevail. They will be utterly ashamed, because they have failed, with an everlasting disgrace that will not be forgotten. Yet, O LORD of hosts, Thou who dost test the righteous, who seest the mind and the heart; let me see Thy vengeance on them; for to Thee I have set forth my cause. Sing to the LORD, praise the LORD! For He has delivered the soul of the needy one from the hand of evildoers.

"The LORD of hosts is with us; the God of Jacob is our stronghold" (Psalm 46:7).

Note

1. Theocracy means that the people are ruled by God; under a monarchy the people are ruled by a king.

DISCUSSION QUESTIONS FOR DAY 34

1. Jehovah-sabaoth is the Lord of hosts. What does it mean?

2. Why do you think God is referred to by this name in Isaiah and Jeremiah and not in Ezekiel?

3. If you had to characterize the strongest quality of Jehovah-sabaoth, what would you say it is?

4. What is the prerequisite for calling on Jehovah-sabaoth? Why?

5. Can you think of a time when you wish you had known this truth about God? When?

6. How did David use this name of God?

7. In what kind of situation can you see that a knowledge of this name would be valuable?

THE
LORD
MY SHEPHERD

DAY THIRTY-FIVE

Have you ever wondered how someone like you has ever survived as well as you have? I have. I once told someone that I was going to write a book entitled, *How to Succeed Though You Fail All the Way!* There are times when I think, "How can someone like me succeed?"

Yet these thoughts don't devastate me because I know where success comes from. It is wonderful to be able to honestly evaluate yourself and not be thrown by the facts. How do I do it? By looking beyond what I am to what my God is and to what that means to me. Do you know what I have discovered? It doesn't matter what I am. It only matters who He is, for He is all I need. He is my Jehovah-raah, the Lord my Shepherd.. And because the Lord is my Shepherd, "I shall not want."

Oh, what a marvelous revelation the Spirit of God gave us as He breathed these words through the pen of David! It's much better than maxims or positive thinking to cling to the precepts of God, for He has magnified His Word above His name (Psalm 138:2).

Can you see the difference? Subtle though it may be, it is the difference between the natural and the spiritual, between our ways and God's ways. To me, positive thinking is humanistic, for even though it gives lip service to God, it still puts man at the center. It says, "Believe in yourself, you can do it." Yet, God's Word says, "For I know nothing good dwells in me" and, "Apart from Me you can do nothing" (Romans 7:18; John 15:5). Rather than believing in myself, seeing my poverty, I turn to His precepts and, with faith in God, say, "I can do all things through Him who strengthens me" (Philippians 4:13). This is to think biblically, to believe what God says.

What does God think about us? Many things, and all of them are precious. "How precious also are Thy thoughts to me, O God! How vast is the sum of them! If I should count them, they would outnumber the sand" (Psalm 139:17-18). Yet, His thoughts are based on an honest evaluation of what we are like.

We are like sheep. Over and over again God refers to us as sheep: "All we like sheep have gone astray" (Isaiah 53:6, KJV). "My sheep hear my voice" (John 10:27, KJV). "We are . . . the sheep of His pasture" (Psalm 100:3). "I . . . will both search my sheep, and seek them out" (Ezekiel 34:11, KJV). "Feed my sheep" (John 21:17, KJV).

164

All the positive maxims in the world can't change the fact that sheep are sheep. What makes the difference in sheep is the shepherd.

Sheep are the dumbest of all animals. They are helpless, timid, and feeble. They require constant attention and meticulous care. Sheep have little means of self-defense. In *How Can I Live,* I wrote these words about sheep:

> If they do not have the constant care of a shepherd, they will go the wrong way, unaware of the dangers at hand. They have been known to nibble themselves right off a mountainside. If they are not led to proper pastures, they will obliviously eat or drink things that are disastrous to them. Not only that, they will literally live their lives in a rut if the shepherd does not lead them to new pastures. Sheep easily fall prey to other animals; when they do, they are virtually defenseless without their shepherd to protect them. Sheep can also become cast down and, in that state, panic and die. And so, because sheep are sheep, they need shepherds to care for them.[1]

Now can you understand why they are sometimes referred to as "dumb sheep"? Why did God create them that way? I believe He had a twofold purpose. First, to show us our total, absolute poverty of spirit, and second, to show us our need of a shepherd. Again I quote from *How Can I Live*:

> The welfare of sheep depends solely upon the care they get from their shepherd. Therefore, the better the shepherd, the better the sheep. When you see sheep that are weak, sickly, and infested with pests, you can be sure that their shepherd really does not care for them. What is our Great Shepherd like? Learn that, and you will understand why you can confidently say,

"The Lord is my shepherd; I shall not want."
Believe it, and you will know a life of perfect
rest. Walk in it, in the obedience of faith, and
you will experience contentment no matter
what your circumstances of life.[2]

Even though we do dumb things, even though we
are not perfect, even though we all stumble in many
ways (James 3:2) we can succeed because the Lord is our
Shepherd. God designed us to be what we are so that
we would see our need of Him. In Him, we find all that
we need. Thus, we can say with total confidence and
conviction, "The LORD is my shepherd, I shall not want"
(Psalm 23:1).

Do you remember what I taught you about observing scripture on pages 113 through 119? Today I want
you to try your hand at observing selected verses from
the tenth chapter of the Gospel of John. Do as much
as you can today. We'll work on it more tomorrow.

As you observe:

1. Mark key repeated words or phrases.

2. Note any contrasts, comparisons, terms of con-
clusions, and/or expressions of time.

3. Constantly ask yourself the five W's and an H.

4. In the right-hand margin, list everything you
learn from the text about:
    a. the sheep
    b. the shepherd
    c. the thief
    d. Jesus
    e. the Father

5. If you have time, pick a favorite verse and mem-
orize it.

JOHN 10:1-17, 26-33

"Truly, truly, I say to you, he who does not enter by the door into the fold of the sheep, but climbs up some other way, he is a thief and a robber. But he who enters by the door is a shepherd of the sheep. To him the doorkeeper opens, and the sheep hear his voice, and he calls his own sheep by name, and leads them out. When he puts forth all his own, he goes before them, and the sheep follow him because they know his voice. And a stranger they simply will not follow, but will flee from him, because they do not know the voice of strangers." This figure of speech Jesus spoke to them, but they did not understand what those things were which He had been saying to them. Jesus therefore said to them again, "Truly, truly, I say to you, I am the door of the sheep. All who came before Me are thieves and robbers, but the sheep did not hear them. I am the door; if anyone enters through Me, he shall be saved, and shall go in and out, and find pasture. The thief comes only to steal, and kill, and destroy; I came that they might have life, and might have *it* abundantly. I am the good shepherd; the good shepherd lays down His life for the sheep. He who is a hireling, and not a shepherd, who is not the owner of the sheep, beholds the wolf coming, and leaves the sheep, and flees, and the wolf snatches them, and scatters *them. He flees* because he is a hireling, and is not concerned about the sheep. I am the good shepherd; and I know My own, and My own know Me, even as the Father knows Me and I know the Father; and I lay down My life for the sheep. And I have other sheep, which are not of this fold; I must bring them also, and they shall hear My voice; and they shall become one flock *with* one shepherd.

For this reason the Father loves Me, because I lay down My life that I may take it again. . . . But you do not believe, because you are not of My sheep. My sheep hear My voice, and I know them, and they follow Me; and I give eternal life to them, and they shall never perish; and no one shall snatch them out of My hand. My Father, who has given *them* to Me, is greater than all; and no one is able to snatch *them* out of the Father's hand. I and the Father are one." The Jews took up stones again to stone Him. Jesus answered them, "I showed you many good works from the Father; for which of them are you stoning Me?" The Jews answered Him, "For a good work we do not stone You, but for blasphemy; and because You, being a man, make Yourself out *to be* God."

Now, one last question. How has God spoken to you today?

DAY THIRTY-SIX

Psalm 23 summarizes one of the greatest truths concerning what it means to be a child of God, to have Him as your Jehovah-raah: "The Lord is my Shepherd, I shall not want."

The rest of the psalm describes why. Read through the psalm written out below and list all that Jehovah-raah does for His sheep. As you read, notice the phrase, "for his name's sake." As your Shepherd, His reputation is at stake, and He cannot fail. Remember, He has magnified His Word above His name (Psalm 138:2). The Word of God stands, because God stands by His Word.

PSALM 23

The LORD is my shepherd; I shall not want. He maketh me to lie down in green pastures; he leadeth me beside the still waters. He restoreth my soul; he leadeth me in the paths of right-eousness for his name's sake. Yea, thou I walk through the valley of the shadow of death, I will fear no evil; for though *art* with me; thy rod and thy staff they comfort me. Thou pre-parest a table before me in the presence of mine enemies; thou anointest my head with oil; my cup runneth over. Surely goodness and mercy shall follow me all the days of my life; and I will dwell in the house of the LORD forever (KJV).

When the psalmist says, "He maketh me to lie down," he is not referring to an enforced rest for the sheep. Rather, he is saying that because the shepherd meets the sheep's needs, the sheep can lie down.

Phillip Keller in his book, *A Shepherd Looks at Psalm 23*, tells us it's impossible for sheep to lie down unless four things are true.

First, sheep must be free from hunger. They cannot lie down as long as they feel a need for finding food. Yet, in the second verse of Psalm 23, we find that the Shepherd has so satisfied the sheep's hunger that they can lie down right in the midst of green pastures. Second, if sheep are to rest, they must be free from fear. Sheep are helpless, timid animals with little means of self-defense. They are easily frightened. Are you, beloved, beset with fears? Third, sheep cannot rest unless they are free from friction. Tension with others of their kind keeps them on their feet, they feel they must defend them-selves! And fourth, sheep cannot rest unless they are free from pests. Sheep can be greatly aggravated and driven to distraction by flies, parasites, or other pests which would seek to torment them.[5]

The Lord My Shepherd

How does your Jehovah-raah shepherd you in regard to these four needs so that you do not want? Read each scripture below. Then, in your own words, summarize how God has made provision for each need.

Need One: Freedom from Hunger

1 PETER 2:2

Like newborn babes, long for the pure milk of the word, that by it you may grow in respect to salvation.

HEBREWS 5:13-14

For everyone who partakes *only* of milk is not accustomed to the word of righteousness, for he is a babe. But solid food is for the mature, who because of practice have their senses trained to discern good and evil.

2 TIMOTHY 3:16-17

All Scripture is inspired by God and profitable for teaching, for reproof, for correction, for training in righteousness; that the man of God may be adequate, equipped for every good work.

DEUTERONOMY 8:3

"And He humbled you and let you be hungry, and fed you with manna which you did not know, nor did your fathers know, that He might make you understand that man does not live by bread alone, but man lives by everything that proceeds out of the mouth of the LORD."

Need Two: Freedom from Fear

1 JOHN 4:16,18

And we have come to know and have believed the love which God has for us. God is love, and the one who abides in love abides in God, and God abides in him. . . . There is no fear in love; but perfect love casts out fear, because fear involves punishment, and the one who fears is not perfected in love.

2 TIMOTHY 1:7

For God has not given us a spirit of timidity, but of power and love and discipline.

PSALM 56:3-4

When I am afraid, I will put my trust in Thee. In God, whose word I praise, in God I have put my trust; I shall not be afraid. What can *mere* man do to me?

Need Three: Freedom from Friction

MATTHEW 6:12,14-15

" 'And forgive us our debts, as we also have forgiven our debtors,' . . . For if you forgive men for their transgressions, your heavenly Father will also forgive you. But if you do not forgive men, then your Father will not forgive your transgressions."

MATTHEW 5:23-24

"If therefore you are presenting your offering at the altar, and there remember that your brother has something against you, leave your offering there before the altar, and go your way; first be reconciled to your brother, and then come and present your offering."

MATTHEW 5:44-45,48

"But I say to you, love your enemies, and pray for those who persecute you in order that you may be sons of your Father who is in heaven; for He causes His sun to rise on *the* evil and *the* good, and sends rain on *the* righteous and *the* unrighteous. . . . Therefore you are to be perfect, as your heavenly Father is perfect."

PHILIPPIANS 2:3-8

Do nothing from selfishness or empty conceit, but with humility of mind let each of you regard one another as more important than himself; do not *merely* look out for your own personal interests, but also for the interests of others. Have this attitude in yourselves which was also in Christ Jesus, who, although He existed in the form of God, did not regard equality with God a thing to be grasped, but emptied Himself, taking the form of a bond-servant, *and* being made in the likeness of men. And being found in appearance as a man, He humbled Himself by becoming obedient to the point of death, even death on a cross.

Need Four: Freedom from Pests

Again, allow me to quote from *How Can I Live*:

Sheep can suffer greatly because of the nose fly. This is a fly that seeks to deposit its eggs on the mucus membrane of the sheep's nose. If this happens the eggs hatch into small worm-like larvae that eventually work their way up the nose into the sheep's head. As these larvae burrow into the sheep's flesh, a tremendous irritation occurs, causing the sheep to thrash and beat its head against anything it can find. A sheep can become so driven to distraction by the irritation that it will actually kill itself in a desperate attempt to get rid of the source of aggravation. As I learned this truth, I could not help but think of so many who are tormented by thoughts that have burrowed their way into their flesh. Eggs have been laid by the enemy and have hatched into repulsive, destructive worms that have worked their way into their heads. Thoughts of fear, rejection, bitterness, hatred, failure, incompetency, sensuality, greed, and more plague God's sheep, tormenting them, driving some even to suicide. But is this to be the fate of God's sheep? No, the Shepherd does have a way to keep His sheep from such torment: "Thou anointest my head with oil" (Psalm 23:5, KJV).[4]

What is the Shepherd's oil of protection against pests that would attack our minds? The following scriptures give us the answer. Read them carefully, and write out in your own words God's instructions that serve as our oil of protection over our minds.

2 CORINTHIANS 10:3-5

For though we walk in the flesh, we do not war according to the flesh, for the weapons of our warfare are not of the flesh, but divinely powerful for the destruction of fortresses. *We are* destroying speculations and every lofty thing raised up against the knowledge of God, and *we are* taking every thought captive to the obedience of Christ.

PHILIPPIANS 4:6-7

Be anxious for nothing, but in everything by prayer and supplication with thanksgiving let your requests be made known to God. And the peace of God, which surpasses all comprehension, shall guard your hearts and your minds in Christ Jesus.

PHILIPPIANS 4:8-9

Finally, brethren, whatever is true, whatever is honorable, whatever is right, whatever is pure, whatever is lovely, whatever is of good repute, if there is any excellence and if anything worthy of praise, let your mind dwell on these things. The things you have learned and received and heard and seen in me, practice these things; and the God of peace shall be with you.

ISAIAH 26:3

"The steadfast of mind Thou wilt keep in perfect peace, because he trusts in Thee."

I want you to note one last truth. It is the end result of having the Lord as your Shepherd:

Surely goodness and lovingkindness will follow me all the days of my life, and I will dwell in the house of the LORD forever (Psalm 23:6).

Notes

1. Kay Arthur, *How Can I Live: A Devotional Journey with Kay Arthur* (Old Tappan, N.J.: Fleming H. Revell Co., 1982), 176.
2. Ibid., 177.
3. Phillip Keller, *A Shepherd Looks at Psalm 23* (Grand Rapids, Mich.: Zondervan Publishing House, 1970.
4. Arthur, *How Can I Live*, 207.

DISCUSSION QUESTIONS FOR DAYS 35 AND 36

1. Because your God is Jehovah-raah, list your benefits as His child, His sheep.

2. What are some of the qualities you have learned about your self as you studied the scriptures on sheep? (Share both the positive and negative.)

3. What is the main responsibility of Jehovah-raah?

4. What did you learn about the four needs of sheep?

5. In what way has Jehovah-raah met your need(s)?

THE LORD OUR RIGHTEOUSNESS

Day Thirty-Seven

Can a man ever really be right with God? "An appalling and horrible thing has happened in the land: the prophets prophesy falsely, and the priests rule on their own authority; and My people love it so!" (Jeremiah 5:30-31). "From the least of them even to the greatest of them, everyone is greedy for gain, and from the prophet even to the priest every one deals falsely. And they have healed the wound of My people, saying, 'Peace, peace,' but there is no peace" (Jeremiah 6:13-14).

Judah had refused to listen to God's words and had walked in the stubbornness of her heart. She had gone after other gods to serve them and bow down to them (Jeremiah 13:10). The whole nation except for a remnant, had corrupted themselves. The corruption was at the top, polluting even the priesthood. No longer could God accept them. He had to call their sins to account (Jeremiah 14:10). Judgment was certain. Nothing except repentance and a return to righteousness could stop it (Jeremiah 18:5-11). Yet when confronted with the option of repentance and righteousness, "they will say, 'It's hopeless! For we are going to follow our own plans, and each of us will act according to the stubbornness of his evil heart' " (Jeremiah 18:12).

Have you ever felt it was hopeless? You had to agree with God. Your heart was deceitful and desperately wicked (Jeremiah 17:9). You knew it. Yet you were going to live the way you wanted to live. Nothing could change it. You were what you were.

Are there some hopeless cases? Helpless victims of their own sinful natures?

When one follows Israel's history to the days of Jeremiah it seems that way. Jehovah had kept His covenant with Abraham (Genesis 15:13-16). He delivered the children of Israel from Egypt just as He said, yet what was the end result? Wandering in the wilderness for forty years because of an evil heart of unbelief (Hebrews 3:12, 16-19).

Finally, under Joshua, they crossed the Jordan and took possession of the land of Canaan. For a while there was victory, victory until the generation who saw the great work which God had done for Israel "were gathered to their fathers" (Judges 2:10). After that "there arose another generation after them who did not know the LORD, nor yet the work which He had done for Israel. Then the sons of Israel did evil in the sight of the LORD, and served the Baals, and they forsook the LORD, the God of their fathers, who had brought them out of the land of Egypt" (Judges 2:10-12).

Three hundred to three hundred and fifty dark years ensued until finally Israel rejected God "from being king over them" (1 Samuel 8:7). They wanted Samuel to appoint a king for them to judge them "like all the nations" (1 Samuel 8:5). So God anointed Saul as king. But Saul "rejected the word of the LORD," so God rejected him from being king (1 Samuel 15:23). Then in mercy God gave them David, a man after His own heart (1 Samuel 13:14; 16:1,11-13), as king. Solomon succeeded David, but "when Solomon was old, his wives turned his heart away after other gods; and his heart was not wholly devoted to the Lord his God . . . and Solomon did what was evil in the sight of the LORD" (1 Kings 11:4,6).

At Solomon's death the kingdom of Israel was divided. Ten tribes under the name Israel set up their capital in Samaria and were known as the Northern Kingdom. The other two tribes, Benjamin and Judah, formed the Southern Kingdom of Judah, and kept Jerusalem as their capital. Of the two kingdoms, Israel was the first to go into captivity. God had had enough of her spiritual harlotries, so He called Assyria to take her captive. "For all the adulteries of faithless Israel" God sent her away and gave "her a writ of divorce, yet her treacherous sister Judah did not fear; but she went and was a harlot also" (Jeremiah 3:8).

This brings us to Jeremiah's day. God spoke through His prophet, saying, "The heart is more deceitful than all else and is desperately sick; who can understand it? I, the LORD, search the heart, I test the mind, even to give to each man according to his ways, according to the results of his deeds" (Jeremiah 17:9-10). God had searched the heart; He had tested the mind. Judgment must now come to Judah.

Are we without hope? Will we always move in this unending cycle? Will the blood of bulls and goats never take away sins (Hebrews 10:3-4)? Can their sacrifices which they offer continually year by year never make them perfect (Hebrews 10:1)? No. Their sacrifices can't make them perfect. Their problem is their heart.

And the blood of bulls and goats can't change a man's heart. Then there is no hope, is there? Yes, there is. And it is in this dark hour of judgment and failure that God reveals to His people another of His names, Jehovah-tsidkenu, the Lord our righteousness. And with that revelation comes the promise of a new covenant, the covenant of grace; and with it a new heart (Jeremiah 31:31-34; Matthew 26:26-28; Hebrews 8:6-13).

These are His sheep—they shall not want, for Jehovah-raah is their Shepherd. As Jehovah-jireh, their Provider, He promises a righteous branch. "This is His name by which He will be called, the Lord our righteousness" (Jeremiah 23:6).

Man can be right with God! To be right with God or to be righteous means to be straight. It is more than goodness. It is to do what God says is right, to live according to His standards. To do so takes a new heart. Man can have a new heart—"I will put My law within them, and on their heart I will write it . . . for I will forgive their iniquity, and their sin I will remember no more" (Jeremiah 31:33-34). "I will put the fear of Me in their hearts so that they will not turn away from Me" (Jeremiah 32:40). "Moreover, I will give you a new heart and put a new spirit within you; and I will remove the heart of stone from your flesh and give you a heart of flesh. And I will put My Spirit within you and cause you to walk in My statutes, and you will be careful to observe My ordinances" (Ezekiel 36:26-27).

All this, a new covenant and, thus, a new heart

will come because of a righteous Branch named Jehovah-tsidkenu, the Lord our righteousness. You can be right with God! You can be righteous. You need not live in an endless cycle of sin and failure. Your heart need not be desperately wicked. You can have a new heart. You need not turn away from Him (Jeremiah 32:40). How? It is all wrapped up in understanding His name, Jehovah-tsidkenu. Let me explain it, precept upon precept. Hang in there, and you will be blessed!

Let me begin by taking you to Jeremiah 23:1-6 where Jehovah-tsidkenu is first used. Read it carefully. As you do, I know you will appreciate the references to shepherds and sheep since we just studied Jehovah-raah.

JEREMIAH 23:1-6

"Woe to the shepherds who are destroying and scattering the sheep of My pasture!" declares the LORD. Therefore thus says the LORD God of Israel concerning the shepherds who are tending My people: "You have scattered My flock and driven them away, and have not attended to them; behold, I am about to attend to you for the evil of your deeds," declares the LORD. "Then I Myself shall gather the remnant of My flock out of all the countries where I have driven them and shall bring them back to their pasture; and they will be fruitful and multiply. I shall also raise up shepherds over them and they will tend them; and they will not be afraid any longer, nor be terrified, nor will any be missing," declares the LORD. "Behold, *the* days are coming," declares the LORD, "when I shall raise up for David a righteous Branch; and He will reign as king and act wisely and do justice and righteousness in the land. In His days Judah will be saved, and Israel will dwell securely; and this is His name by which He will be called, 'The LORD our righteousness.' "

Now before we proceed, let me ask you a few questions:

1. Today's lesson began with a description of the condition of Judah during Jeremiah's time. Who were the bad shepherds that the Lord was speaking about in Jeremiah 23?

2. What happened to "my flock"?

3. What is the Lord going to do for His flock? List every insight you can glean from Jeremiah 23:1-6.

4. When God referred to David (v. 5), to whom was He actually referring?

5. List all you observe from this text about the "righteous Branch."

6. Who do you think this "righteous Branch" is?

DAY THIRTY-EIGHT

In 1 Kings 2:1-4, as "David's time to die drew near," he told Solomon of God's promise to him—"you shall not lack a man on the throne of Israel." God's Word to David was certain, "Your kingdom shall endure before Me forever; your throne shall be established forever" (2 Samuel 7:16). The righteous Branch in Jeremiah 23:5 is the fulfillment of God's promise to David. The righteous Branch who will reign as king and do justice and righteousness in the land is God incarnate (God in the flesh), the Messiah, the Lord Jesus Christ, our righteousness.

The descendant of David by Mary would grow up as a "root out of a dry ground" (Isaiah 53:2, KJV) and

182

the Lord would cause "the iniquity of us all to fall on Him" (Isaiah 53:6). He would be the sinless Lamb of God that would "save His people from their sins" (Matthew 1:21; 1 Peter 1;18-19). He was "pierced through for our transgressions . . . crushed for our iniquities; the chastening for our well-being fell upon Him, and by His scourging we are healed" of our sins (Isaiah 53:5; 1 Peter 2:24-25).

But would forgiveness of sins be enough? No. Listen carefully to what Jesus said in the Sermon on the Mount. "For I say to you, that unless your righteousness surpasses that of the scribes and Pharisees, you shall not enter the kingdom of heaven" (Matthew 5:20).

But how could our righteousness exceed the righteousness of the scribes and Pharisees when "all our righteousnesses are as filthy rags" (Isaiah 64:6, KJV) and "there is none righteous, no, not one" (Romans 3:10, KJV). If "all have sinned, and come short of the glory of God" (Romans 3:23, KJV), where then can a man obtain righteousness, or how can a man be made righteousness?

At Calvary's cross "He made Him who knew no sin to be sin on our behalf, that we might become the righteousness of God in Him" (2 Corinthians 5:21)— "even the righteousness of God through faith in Jesus Christ for all those who believe" (Romans 3:22).

There He hung, Jehovah-tsidkenu, made sin for you, so that you, by believing in Him, might be made His righteousness.

ROMANS 6:16

Do you not know that when you present yourselves to someone as slaves for obedience, you are slaves of the one whom you obey, either of sin resulting in death, or of obedience resulting in righteousness?

My friend, have you become "obedient from the heart to that form of teaching to which you were committed (Romans 6:17), the gospel of Jesus Christ? If so, you have "been freed from sin" (sin's reign) (Romans 6:18) and have become "slaves of righteousness" (Romans 6:18). You have been given a new heart, a heart of flesh, not of stone (2 Corinthians 3:3; Ezekiel 36:26). You have a new master. His name is Adonai, your Jehovah-tsidkenu. Hallelujah, what a name!

Down through the ages, from the sacrifice God made in the Garden of Eden to provide a covering for the nakedness of Adam and Eve's sin, to the passover lamb which brought deliverance from Egypt, to the temple sacrifices of the blood of innocent bulls and goats, sinful man has seen that the death of the innocent is required for the guilty. Yet the blood of bulls and goats could not take away sins or sprinkle clean their hearts from an evil conscience (Hebrews 10:22).

Therefore, when He comes into the world, He says, "SACRIFICE AND OFFERING THOU HAST NOT DESIRED, BUT A BODY THOU HAST PREPARED FOR ME; IN WHOLE BURNT OFFERINGS AND *sacrifices* FOR SIN THOU HAS TAKEN NO PLEASURE. THEN I SAID, 'BEHOLD, I HAVE COME TO DO THY WILL O GOD.'" After saying above, "SACRIFICES AND OFFERINGS AND WHOLE BURNT OFFERINGS AND *sacrifices* FOR SIN THOU HAS NOT DESIRED, NOR HAST THOU TAKEN PLEASURE *in them*" (which are offered according to the Law), then He said, "BEHOLD, I HAVE COME TO DO THY WILL." He takes away the first in order to establish the second. By this will we have been sanctified through the offering of the body of Jesus Christ once for all (Hebrews 10:5-10).

Sanctified and made righteous.

Can we be right with God? Only by receiving the Lord Jesus Christ. "But as many as received Him, to them He gave the right to become children of God, even to those who believe in His name" (John 1:12). "You shall call His name Jesus, for it is He who will save His people from their sins" (Matthew 1:21).

Are you right with God? "Blessed are they who do hunger and thirst after righteousness; for they shall be filled" (Matthew 5:6, KJV).

1. What was the promise that came with the revelation of God as Jehovah-tsidkenu?

2. What were the benefits of the promise?

3. What insights did you gain about the righteous Branch?

a. Who was He?

b. What difference does that make in your life?

THE LORD IS THERE

DAY THIRTY-NINE

What do you do when you feel alone? Abandoned? Forgotten by everyone—maybe even God? What do you do when an iron bolt slides shut, imprisoning you in difficult circumstances? What do you do? How do you survive?

When the bolt slid into the iron casing on Geoffrey Bull's cell door, he didn't know he would be shut up as a prisoner for the next three years. Taken prisoner by Chinese Communists, he was in the grip of determined atheists, men who hated all that Geoffrey lived for. Their goal was either to correct his thinking and reform him or torture and kill him. How would he survive an undetermined prison sentence? How would he take solitary confinement? How would he keep his sanity when his body would be mercilessly tortured over and over again. His life seemed hell on earth—how could the joy of the Lord be his strength? He could continue to believe in God because he knew God's name, Jehovah-shammah, the Lord is there.

In his book, *God Holds the Key,* Geoffrey Bull writes:

> I had no Bible in my hand, no watch on my wrist, no pencil or paper in my pocket. There was no real hope of release. There was no real hope of life. There was no real possibility of reunion with those I loved. The only reality was my Lord and Saviour Jesus Christ. Divested of all, He was to become everything to me. He was to break my bars and enlarge my coasts in the narrow room. He was to be my fullest nourishment amidst the meager food. "My meat," which my captors "knew not of." He would make me glad with His countenance. He would let me hear His voice. As in the days of His nativity, Herod may reign and imagine slaughter against the innocent but let me only see His star and I would come to worship Him. . . .

The exile need not be servile. God makes His children kings and priests however small the immediate domain. . . . My portion was to be in the contemplation of the Lord of glory in the secret place; to gain a real experience in the contemplative content of the Christian faith, which centuries have stolen from our western lives. . . . To see the King in His beauty must be our one desiring; to hunger, thirst and take our fill of Him. And if He makes us stand in some obscure and darkened corner of His palace yard, we can be sure He puts us there because from that distinct advantage we, with our present stature, will behold Him best whenever He comes passing by. "A day in Thy courts," they used to sing, "is better than a thousand," and many would have given everything, to be some humble doorkeeper in the house of the Lord.[1]

The children of Israel were in captivity. They would be there seventy years (Jeremiah 29:10). They, too, would have gladly been a doorkeeper in the house of the Lord, if He had been there. But He was not. They had heard from Ezekiel how the glory of the Lord had departed from the temple (Ezekiel 10:18-19; 11:22-24). It was hard for them to believe. However, captivity was necessary, for, as you just read, God had to judge His people for their adultery. From captivity in Egypt to captivity in Babylon, God would teach hard but needful lessons. Among those lessons would be another truth about Himself through His name, Jehovah-shammah, the Lord is there.

Jehovah-shammah is found in the last verse of Ezekiel where it is used in reference to the earthly Jerusalem, the city which the Lord Jesus Christ will inhabit when He returns to earth to reign as King of kings and Lord of lords. "The city shall be 18,000 cubits round about; and the name of the city from that day shall be, 'The LORD is there' " (Ezekiel 48:35). The word *shammah* is simply the word for *there*. Remember, in biblical times a name usually described the character of the one who bore it. Therefore, when God named this city Jehovah-shammah, He was assuring His people that He, Jehovah, would be there. Oh, what a message of encouragement this was to those in captivity! It assured them of a future and gave them hope.

We need a future and a hope. Our world, for the most part, lives for today. "Give it to me now!" To most people, the future seems so uncertain, so hopeless that people have lost their vision and live only for their immediate happiness. Without a vision the people perish (Proverbs 29:18).

This is what happened in the Korean War. The majority of our men who were taken captive never tried to escape. This was unprecedented, especially in comparison to World War II. They were resigned to prison because they saw no future; they had lost their vision; their hope was gone. They gave in and were absorbed by their captivity. This is what has happened to many Christians. They have lost sight of the blessed hope, the glory of being absent from the body and at home with the Lord, the time when they will reign with Jesus on earth (Daniel 7:27). They have lost their will to fight because they have forgotten that their "citizenship is in heaven" (Philippians 3:20). They have sat down at the world's banquet table and glutted themselves with the things of this life. They have little interest in the glories of heaven. They can see and touch and taste and experience "now," but they can't fathom the glories that are yet to come. Many Christians have become prisoners who will not try to escape. They are no threat to the world which holds them captive.

How can a Christian keep from being changed by the world? How can we keep our vision and not lose hope? By obedience to God's Word, by clinging to it in faith. Carefully read the following scriptures. Then write in your own words a practical way you could put that truth into practice, or record what would be required of you if you were to live according to that truth. What would you have to change, to stop, to start doing? Write it down. Look at it. Then decide what you will do about it.

COLOSSIANS 3:1-2

If then you have been raised up with Christ, keep seeking the things above, where Christ is, seated at the right hand of God. Set your mind on the things above, not on the things that are on earth.

PHILIPPIANS 3:7-8

But whatever things were gain to me, those things I have counted as loss for the sake of Christ. More than that, I count all things to be loss in view of the surpassing value of knowing Christ Jesus my Lord, for whom I have suffered the loss of all things, and count them but rubbish in order that I may gain Christ.

1 THESSALONIANS 1:9-10

For they themselves report about us what kind of a reception we had with you, and how you turned to God from idols to serve a living and true God, and to wait for His Son from heaven, whom He raised from the dead, *that is* Jesus, who delivers us from the wrath to come.

2 TIMOTHY 2:3-4

Suffer hardship with *me*, as a good soldier of Christ Jesus. No soldier in active service entangles himself in the affairs of everyday life, so that he may please the one who enlisted him as a soldier.

2 CORINTHIANS 4:11,16-18

For we who live are constantly being delivered over to death for Jesus' sake, that the life of Jesus also may be manifested in our mortal flesh . . . Therefore we do not lose heart, but though our outer man is decaying, yet our inner man is being renewed day by day. For momentary, light affliction is producing for us an eternal weight of glory far beyond all comparison, while we look not at the things which are seen, but at the things which are not seen;

for the things which are seen are temporal, but the things which are not seen are eternal.

HEBREWS 11:25-27

Choosing rather to endure ill-treatment with the people of God, than to enjoy the passing pleasures of sin; considering the reproach of Christ greater riches than the treasures of Egypt; for he was looking to the reward. By faith he left Egypt, not fearing the wrath of the king; for he endured, as seeing Him who is unseen.

Wherever you are, my friend, Jehovah is there. Waiting, longing to be your future and your hope. Do not be absorbed by your captivity; rather, be absorbed with your God. "Whom have I in heaven but Thee? And besides Thee, I desire nothing on earth. My flesh and my heart may fail; but God is the strength of my heart and my portion forever. For, behold, those who are far from Thee will perish; Thou hast destroyed all those who are unfaithful to Thee. But as for me, the nearness of God is my good; I have made the LORD God my refuge, that I may tell of all Thy works" (Psalm 73:25-28).

Jehovah-shammah—we will talk more of Him tomorrow.

DAY FORTY

I long to have the watchword of the church once again become, Maranatha, the Lord is coming. What will it take? Will it take the same thing it took with God's chosen people, Israel and Judah? Before they were ever taken captive into Babylon, they were taken captive by the world. Their captivity in Babylon was God's doing because they chose the world over Him.

As God's heart ached over them, does it ache for the church today? Listen to His pain and their judgment. Can you see the possibility of anything similar happening to your country?

EZEKIEL 6:9-7:7

"How I have been hurt by their adulterous hearts which turned away from Me, and by their eyes, which played the harlot after their idols; and they will loathe themselves in their own sight for the evils which they have committed, for all their abominations. Then they will know that I am the LORD; I have not said in vain that I would inflict this disaster on them." Thus says the Lord GOD, "Clap your hand, stamp your foot, and say 'Alas, because of all the evil abominations of the house of Israel, which will fall by sword, famine, and plague! He who is far off will die by the plague, and he who is near will fall by the sword, and he who remains and is besieged will die by the famine. Thus shall I spend My wrath on them. Then you will know that I am the LORD, when their slain are among their idols around their altars, on every high hill, on all the tops of the mountains, under every green tree, and under every leafy oak—the places where they offered soothing aroma to all their idols. So throughout all their habitations I shall stretch out My hand against them and make the land more desolate and waste than the wilderness toward Diblah; thus they will know that I am the LORD.' " Moreover, the word of the LORD came to me saying, "And you, son of man, thus says the Lord GOD to the land of Israel, 'An end! The end is coming on the four corners of the land. Now the end is upon you, and I shall send My anger against you; I shall judge you according to your ways, and I shall bring all your

193

abominations upon you. For My eye will have no pity on you, nor shall I spare *you,* but I shall bring your ways upon you, and your abominations will be among you; then you will know that I am the LORD!' Thus says the Lord GOD, 'A disaster, unique disaster, behold it is coming! An end is coming; the end has come! It has awakened against you; behold, it has come! Your doom has come to you, O inhabitant of the land. The time has come, the day is near—tumult rather than joyful shouting on the mountains.' "

The background and setting for Ezekiel is this: Ezekiel is a captivity book—written to those Jews who had been taken captive into Babylon. However, as Ezekiel opens, Jerusalem still had not been destroyed. There were three invasions on Jerusalem before its fall. Daniel was taken captive in the first invasion and Ezekiel, in the second. As you read Ezekiel, you must keep in mind that at the beginning of his prophecy, Jerusalem still stood.

You find Ezekiel prophesying Jerusalem's fall. During this time Ezekiel records the glory of the Lord departing from the temple (Ezekiel 10-11). Then Jerusalem fell (Ezekiel 33:21).

Ezekiel was deported to Babylon in 597 B.C., along with King Jehoiachin and hosts of citizens, when Nebuchadnezzar invaded Jerusalem the second time (read 2 Kings 24:10-16). Ezekiel was not called to prophesy until after he had been in Babylonia for about five years. . . . The idolatry which Ezekiel saw as Judah's blight before he left Jerusalem was the same condition he faced in the settlements of Jewish exiles in Babylonia. The judgment of captivity did not stir the first contingents of

exiles to repentance. In fact, they found it very
hard to believe, as Ezekiel was prophesying,
that Jerusalem would actually be destroyed by
the Babylonians. They were loath to believe
that Jehovah had given world dominion to
Babylon. Hence, it was necessary for Ezekiel in
Babylon—and Jeremiah in Jerusalem—to show
the people how unfounded were any expecta-
tions of immediate deliverance.[2]

According to Irving Jensen, the book of Ezekiel
can be divided into two main parts: chapters 1-32 is
"Jehovah Not There" and chapters 33-48 is "Jehovah
There."

There is a turning point in the book, made up
of two parts. At 24:2, Ezekiel is informed by
God that the king of Babylon has begun the
siege against Jerusalem. At 33:21, the actual
turning point, Ezekiel learns from a messenger
that the city has fallen. Up to 24:2, Ezekiel's
message is mainly "The city shall be
destroyed." After 33:21, Ezekiel looks to the
next prophetic peak, and prophesies, "The city
shall be restored." It is at chapter 24 that the
prophet learns that when Jerusalem falls, his
tongue will be loosed to speak a new message
of hope; and people, sobered by the reality of
Jerusalem's destruction, will begin to give him
a hearing.[3]

News of the destruction of Jerusalem comes in
Ezekiel 33:21: "Now it came about in the twelfth year
of our exile, on the fifth of the tenth month, that the
refugees from Jerusalem came to me, saying, 'The city
has been taken.' "

It was difficult for God's people to believe He would
let Jerusalem fall. Yet they forgot another of God's

names. It is a name that I never hear anyone mention: Jealous, Qanna. When God gave the Ten Commandments, He said:

EXODUS 20:1-6

Then God spoke all these words, saying, "I am the LORD your God, who brought you out of the land of Egypt, out of the house of slavery. You shall have no other gods before Me. You shall not make for yourself an idol, or any likeness of what is in heaven above or on the earth beneath or in the water under the earth. You shall not worship them or serve them; for I, the LORD your God, am a jealous God, visiting the iniquity of the fathers on the children, on the third and the fourth generations of those who hate Me, but showing lovingkindness to thousands, to those who love Me and keep My commandments."

In Exodus 34:14, God Himself said that His name is Jealous. Listen to how He told them.

EXODUS 34:12-17

Watch yourself that you make no covenant with the inhabitants of the land into which you are going, lest it become a snare in your midst. But *rather,* you are to tear down their altars and smash their *sacred* pillars and cut down their Asherim—for you shall not worship any other god, for the LORD, whose name is Jealous, is a jealous God—lest you make a covenant with the inhabitants of the land and they play the harlot with their gods, and sacrifice to their gods, and someone invite you to eat of his sacrifice; and you take some of his daughters for your sons, and his daughters play the harlot with their gods, and cause your sons *also* to play the harlot with their gods. You shall make for yourself no molten gods.

There is a holy and godly jealousy (2 Corinthians 11:2) and God acted according to His name, just as He had warned His people He would. He left Jerusalem.

So that the sequence of events might be established in your mind, answer the following questions. Tomorrow we'll continue our study of God's name, Jehovah-shammah.

1. What does God call a person who worships idols?

2. What evils had God's people committed?

3. How did their actions affect God? Why?

4. How did God judge Israel and Judah for their idolatry?

5. Did God's people expect this type of judgment? Why?

6. Match the following:

a. Ezekiel 33:21   _____ 1. Hebrew word for jealous
b. Jeremiah   _____ 2. Jehovah There
c. Ezekiel 1-32   _____ 3. Jehovah Not There
d. Daniel   _____ 4. Taken captive during Jerusalem's first invasion
e. Ezekiel 1-24
f. Assyrians
g. Jerusalem   _____ 5. Taken captive during Jerusalem's second invasion
h. Qanna
i. Ezekiel 10-11
j. Babylonians   _____ 6. Remained in Jerusalem through all three invasions
k. Ezekiel
l. Ezekiel 33-48

197

m. Jehovah-shammah _____ 7. Jerusalem still
n. Jehovah-tsidkenu standing
o. Amos _____ 8. God's presence
leaves Temple, then
Jerusalem
_____ 9. Jerusalem fallen (third
invasion)
____10. People who
destroyed Jerusalem
____11. God's way of promis
ing to return to
Jerusalem
____12. A city made desolate
waste because of
God's jealousy

7. Do you think God's character has changed since
the days of Ezekiel? Explain your answer.

8. How can you apply what you have learned today
to your own life? Answer in the first person—"I . . ."

DAY FORTY-ONE

God had always been with Israel and Judah, manifesting His presence in one way or another. Yet it
seems, for the most part, they took His presence for
granted, so much so that they couldn't believe He
would do what He said He would do. They couldn't
believe He would depart and let Jerusalem, God's
earthly Zion, be taken captive by the ungodly
Babylonians.

Some scriptures show how God let them know He
was present with them. As you look at each, note the
form that His presence took; record this along with
any other pertinent insights below each section of
scripture.

EXODUS 13:20-22

Then they set out from Succoth and camped in Etham on the edge of the wilderness. And the LORD was going before them in a pillar of cloud by day to lead them on the way, and in a pillar of fire by night to give them light, that they might travel by day and by night. He did not take away the pillar of cloud by day, nor the pillar of fire by night, from before the people.

EXODUS 23:20-22

Behold, I am going to send an angel before you to guard you along the way, and to bring you into the place which I have prepared. Be on your guard before him and obey his voice; do not be rebellious toward him, for he will not pardon your transgression, since My name is in him. But if you will truly obey his voice and do all that I say, then I will be an enemy to your enemies and an adversary to your adversaries.

EXODUS 33:12-16

Then Moses said to the LORD, "See, Thou dost say to me, 'Bring up this people!' But Thou Thyself hast not let me know whom Thou wilt send with me. Moreover, Thou hast said, 'I have known you by name, and you have also found favor in My sight.' Now therefore, I pray Thee, if I have found favor in Thy sight, let me know Thy ways, that I may know Thee, so that I may find favor in Thy sight. Consider too, that this nation is Thy people." And He said, "My presence shall go *with you,* and I will give you rest." Then he said to Him, "If Thy presence does not go *with us,* do not lead us up from here. For how then can it be known that I have found favor in Thy sight, I and Thy people? Is it not by Thy going with us, so that we, I and Thy people, may be distinguished from all the *other* people who are upon the face of the earth?"

Exodus 40:34-38

Then the cloud covered the tent of meeting, and the glory of the LORD filled the tabernacle. And Moses was not able to enter the tent of meeting because the cloud had settled on it, and the glory of the LORD filled the tabernacle. And throughout all their journeys whenever the cloud was taken up from over the tabernacle, the sons of Israel would set out; but if the cloud was not taken up, then they did not set out until the day when it was taken up. For throughout all their journeys, the cloud of the LORD was on the tabernacle by day, and there was fire in it by night, in the sight of all the house of Israel.

Deuteronomy 4:37

Because He loved your fathers, therefore He chose their descendants after them. And He personally [literally, with His presence] brought you from Egypt by His great power.

JOSHUA 1:1-2,5

Now it came about after the death of Moses the servant of the LORD that the LORD spoke to Joshua the son of Nun, Moses' servant, saying, "Moses My servant is dead; now therefore arise, cross this Jordan, you and all this people, . . . No man will *be able* to stand before you all the days of your life. Just as I have been with Moses, I will be with you; I will not fail you or forsake you."

JOSHUA 5:13-15

Now it came about when Joshua was by Jericho, that he lifted up his eyes and looked, and behold, a man was standing opposite him with his sword drawn in his hand, and Joshua went to him and said to him, "Are you for us or for our adversaries?" And he said, "No, rather, I indeed come now *as* captain of the host of the LORD." And Joshua fell on his face to the earth, and bowed down, and said to him, "What has my lord to say to his servant?" And the captain of the LORD's host said to Joshua, "Remove your sandals from your feet, for the place where you are standing is holy." And Joshua did so.

JUDGES 6:14-16

And the LORD looked at him and said, "Go in this your strength and deliver Israel from the hand of Midian. Have I not sent you?" And he said to Him, "O Lord, how shall I deliver Israel? Behold, my family is the least in Manasseh, and I am the youngest in my father's house." But the LORD said to him, "Surely I will be with you, and you shall defeat Midian as one man."

1 SAMUEL 4:6-7

And when the Philistines heard the noise of the shout, they said, "What *does* the noise of this great shout in the camp of the Hebrews *mean?*" Then they understood that the ark of the LORD had come into the camp. And the Philistines were afraid, for they said, "God has come into the camp." And they said, "Woe to us! For nothing like this has happened before."

ISAIAH 63:9

In all their affliction He was afflicted, and the angel of His presence saved them; in His love and in His mercy He redeemed them; and He lifted them and carried them all the days of old.

PSALM 132:8,13-14

Arise, O LORD, to Thy resting place; Thou and the ark of Thy strength. . . . For the LORD has chosen Zion; He has desired it for His habitation. "This is My resting place forever; here I will dwell, for I have desired it."

2 CHRONICLES 7:1-5

[Solomon had just finished building the temple in Jerusalem.] Now when Solomon had finished

praying, fire came down from heaven and consumed the burnt offering and the sacrifices; and the glory of the LORD filled the house. And the priests could not enter into the house of the LORD, because the glory of the LORD filled the LORD's house. And all the sons of Israel, seeing the fire come down and the glory of the LORD upon the house, bowed down on the pavement with their faces to the ground, and they worshiped and gave praise to the LORD, *saying,* "Truly He is good, truly His lovingkindness is everlasting." Then the king and all the people offered sacrifice before the LORD. And King Solomon offered a sacrifice of 22,000 oxen, and 120,000 sheep. Thus the king and all the people dedicated the house of God.

This brings us to the time of Jeremiah and Ezekiel who were, for a while, contemporaries. While Ezekiel was in captivity, Jeremiah was in Jerusalem where he witnessed and survived all three Babylonian invasions.

Let's begin with some verses that show Jehovah-shammah, His presence in the inner court in Jerusalem. As you read this first scripture underline what caused the Lord such grief. Write it out below.

EZEKIEL 8:3-6, 17-18

And He stretched out the form of a hand and caught me by a lock of my head; and the Spirit lifted me up between earth and heaven and brought me in the visions of God to Jerusalem, to the entrance of the north gate of the inner *court,* where the seat of the idol of jealousy, which provokes to jealousy, was *located.* And behold, the glory of the God of Israel *was* there, like the appearance which I saw in the plain. Then He said to me, "Son of man, raise your eyes, now, toward the north." So I raised my eyes toward the north, and behold, to the north of the altar gate *was* this idol of jealousy at the entrance. And He said to me, "Son of man, do you see what they are doing, the great abominations which the house of Israel are committing here, that I should be far from My sanctuary? But yet you will see still greater abominations." . . . And He said to me, "Do you see *this*, son of man? Is it too light a thing for the house of Judah to commit the abominations which they have committed here, that they have filled the land with violence and provoked Me repeatedly? For behold, they are putting the twig to their nose. Therefore, I indeed shall deal in wrath. My eye will have no pity nor shall I spare; and though they cry in My ears with a loud voice, yet I shall not listen to them."

Ezekiel 10:3-4

[Here the Lord was standing over the threshold of His house.] Now the cherubim were standing on the right side of the temple when the man entered, and the cloud filled the inner court. Then the glory of the LORD went up from the cherub to the threshold of the temple, and the temple was filled with the cloud, and the court was filled with the brightness of the glory of the LORD.

Ezekiel 10:18

[Then He moved and stood over the cherubim.] Then the glory of the LORD departed from the threshold of the temple and stood over the cherubim.

EZEKIEL 10:19

[Next He was at the door of the east gate.] When the cherubim departed, they lifted their wings and rose up from the earth in my sight with the wheels beside them; and they stood still at the entrance of the east gate of the LORD's house. And the glory of the God of Israel hovered over them.

EZEKIEL 11:22-23

[Finally God paused on the Mount of Olives, east of Jerusalem.] Then the cherubim lifted up their wings with the wheels beside them, and the glory of the God of Israel hovered over them. And the glory of the LORD went up from the midst of the city, and stood over the mountain which is east of the city.

Can you sense the Lord's reluctance in leaving His temple, His city where He had set His name? Do you see Him lingering, longingly waiting for her cry of repentance? This, Beloved, is our God whose name is Jealous. He will not have any other gods before Him.

Although God left Jerusalem, He had to come back, for He is Jehovah, a covenant-keeping God. Even as God prepared to leave Jerusalem in Ezekiel 11:22-24, Ezekiel fell on his face and cried, "Alas, Lord GOD! Wilt Thou bring the remnant of Israel to a complete end?" (Ezekiel 11:13). Listen to Jehovah's response:

Therefore say, "Thus says the Lord GOD, 'Though I had removed them far away among the nations, and though I had scattered them among the countries, yet I was a sanctuary for them a little while in the countries where they had gone.' " Therefore say, "Thus says the Lord GOD, 'I shall gather you from the peoples and assemble you out of the countries among which you have been scattered, and I shall give you the land of Israel.' " When they come there, they will remove all its detestable things and all its abominations from it. And I shall give them one heart, and shall put a new spirit within them. And I shall take the heart of stone out of their flesh and give them a heart of flesh. (Ezekiel 11:16-19).

Now you can understand how much it meant to God's people when God said, "The city shall be 18,000 cubits round about; and the name of the city from that day shall be, 'The Lord is there' " (Ezekiel 48:35). Jehovah would return.

Maranatha, The Lord is coming! Are you expecting Him? Are you ready? We shall discuss it more tomorrow.

DAY FORTY-TWO

The hope—the promise of His return—was Israel's. However, it would be approximately six hundred years before the Lord would come to His temple. And even when that happened, it would not be the complete fulfillment of Ezekiel 48:35: "The name of the city from that day shall be, 'The Lord is there,' " Jehovah-shammah. (At the end of Day 42, see the chart of God's plan of the ages. You will want to study this chart so that you can see when Jesus will return to set up His reign and dwell in Jerusalem.)

After seventy years of captivity, a remnant would return to Jerusalem. Under Ezra and Zerubbabel, they would rebuild the temple; under Nehemiah, they would rebuild the walls of Jerusalem. Yet they would weep, for the second temple could not compare with the glory of Solomon's temple. Neither could this rebuilt Jerusalem equal Jerusalem in her former days. Sin costs. It always does. Yes, there is forgiveness with God. "The LORD's lovingkindnesses indeed never cease, for His compassions never fail" (Lamentations 3:22); however, sin does have its own harvest.

Although the Lord did not return to dwell in His Shekinah glory in His temple at Jerusalem, He confirmed His promise of Ezekiel 48:35 through Zechariah, a post-exilic prophet. "'Sing for joy and be glad, O daughter of Zion; for behold I am coming and I will dwell in your midst,' declares the LORD. 'And many nations will join themselves to the LORD in that day and will become My people. Then I will dwell in your midst, and you will know that the LORD of hosts has sent Me to you. And the LORD will possess Judah as His portion in the holy land, and will again choose Jerusalem. Be silent, all flesh, before the LORD; for He is aroused from His holy habitation'" (Zechariah 2:10-13).

Dwell is the root word from which we get *Shekinah,* signifying the dwelling presence of the Lord on earth. God also spoke again through that final Old Testament prophet, Malachi. "Behold, I am going to send My messenger, and he will clear the way before Me. And the Lord, whom you seek, will suddenly come to His temple; and the messenger of the covenant, in whom you delight, behold, He is coming,' says the LORD of hosts" (Malachi 3:1). But that was all God said. Malachi was the last of the Old Testament prophets. They would not hear another word from God for four hundred years. During that time the children of Israel had two things to cling to: His name, Jehovah-shammah, and His Word which He magnified above His name (Psalm 138:2).

These two things are seen in Ezekiel 39:25-29:

Therefore thus says the Lord GOD, "Now I shall restore the fortunes of Jacob, and have mercy on the whole house of Israel; and I shall be jealous for My holy name. And they shall forget their disgrace and all their treachery which they perpetrated against Me, when they live securely on their *own* land with no one to make them afraid. When I bring them back from the peoples and gather them from the lands of their enemies, then I shall be sanctified through them in the sight of the many nations. Then they will know that I am the LORD their God because I made them go into exile among the nations, and then gathered them *again* to their own land; and I will leave none of them there any longer. And I will not hide My face from them any longer, for I shall have poured out My Spirit on the house of Israel," declares the Lord GOD.

Because God was jealous for His Holy Name, because His Word stands above His name, He would return, in His glory, to Jerusalem.[4]

And He did, but most of Israel did not believe it was He. He came to His own, but His own received Him not (John 1:11). "In the beginning was the Word, and the Word was with God, and the Word was God. . . . And the Word became flesh, and dwelt among us, and we beheld His glory, glory as of the only begotten from the Father, full of grace and truth" (John 1:1, 14).

In the Greek, *dwelt* is translated "tabernacled." Jesus, the "Mighty God, Eternal Father, Prince of Peace" (Isaiah 9:6), came to Jerusalem. Simeon recognized Him when He was brought as an infant to be presented "to the Lord" (Luke 2:22).

He took Him into his arms, and blessed God, and said, "Now Lord, Thou dost let Thy bond-servant depart in peace, according to Thy word; for my eyes have seen Thy salvation, which Thou hast prepared in the presence of all peoples, a LIGHT OF REVELATION TO THE GENTILES, and the glory of Thy people Israel" (Luke 2:28-32).

Scripture tells us He came again to the temple when He was twelve. Although the Jews were impressed, they didn't realize they were listening to Jehovah-shammah begin His ministry among them (Luke 3:23). They saw His miracles and heard His words; but didn't believe. Instead of believing He was Jehovah, I AM, "they picked up stones to throw at Him; but Jesus hid Himself, and went out of the temple" (John 8:59). They refused to submit to Adonai. They could not see that it was Jehovah-jireh who stood before them in the temple. There, on Mount Moriah, in the very place where Abraham offered a ram instead of Isaac, stood the Lamb of God, God's provision for their sins. But they were stubborn and blind. They stopped up their ears and closed their eyes (Matthew 13:13-15). They refused to follow Jehovah-raah, the Shepherd that would give them life.

"As a result of this many of His disciples withdrew, and were not walking with Him any more" (John 6:66). They would not rally around Jehovah-nissi, their standard. "For not knowing about God's righteousness, and seeking to establish their own, they did not subject themselves to the righteousness of God" (Romans 10:3). "For Christ [Jehovah-tsidkenu] is the end of the law for righteousness to everyone who believes" (Romans 10:4). But they refused to believe.

When the Jews plotted to take His life and arrest Jesus in the garden of Gethsemane, they never dreamed they were laying their hands on Jehovah-sabaoth, the Lord of hosts, who could have at His "disposal more than twelve legions of angels" (Matthew 26:53). They crucified Jehovah-tsidkenu. As the blood and water poured forth, they didn't know it was the balm of Gilead, the blood of Jehovah-rapha, the Lord that healeth. Nor could they believe that "by one offering He has perfected for all time those who are sanctified" (Hebrews 10:14). Those who wanted to be holy didn't see it was Jehovah-mekoddishkem who hung on that cross for their sanctification. Thus, they missed "peace with God through our Lord Jesus Christ," Jehovah-shalom (Romans 5:1). Yet Jesus had done what He said, "I have made Thy name known to them, and will make it known" (John 17:26).

He was in Palestine for thirty-three years going in and out of the temple. Then one day the glory of the Lord again departed from the temple, saying. "O Jerusalem, Jerusalem, who kills the prophets and stones those who are sent to her! How often I wanted to gather your children together, the way a hen gathers her chicks under her wings, and you were unwilling. Behold, your house is being left to you desolate! For I say to you, from now on you shall not see Me until you say, 'BLESSED IS HE WHO COMES IN THE NAME OF THE LORD! And Jesus came out from the temple" (Matthew 23:37-24:1).

Jesus went to be with the Father, but He did not leave us comfortless. Even now He is Jehovah-shammah to those who have believed on His name, for He dwells within. "But I tell you the truth, it is to your advantage that I go away; for if I do not go away, the Helper shall not come to you; but if I go, I will send Him to you" (John 16:7).

We who have believed on the name of the Lord Jesus Christ, "do you not know that you are a temple of God, and that the Spirit of God dwells in you" (1 Corinthians 3:16)? It is "Christ in you, the hope of glory" (Colossians 1:27). "He Himself has said, 'I WILL NEVER DESERT YOU, NOR WILL I EVER FORSAKE YOU'" (Hebrews 13:5).

And how then are we to live? We are to live in the

expectancy of "His Son from heaven, whom He raised from the dead, that is Jesus, who delivers us from the wrath to come" (1 Thessalonians 1:9-10).

God promised He would return to Jerusalem and that the name of Jerusalem would be Jehovah-shammah, the Lord is there. When He returns, then His word through Ezekiel to His people Israel will be fulfilled.

> And say to them, "Thus says the Lord God, 'Behold, I will take the sons of Israel from among the nations where they have gone, and I will gather them from every side and bring them into their own land; and I will make them one nation in the land, on the mountain of Israel; and one king will be king for all of them; and they will no longer be two nations, and they will no longer be divided into two Kingdoms. And they will no longer defile themselves with their idols, or with their detestable things, or with any of their transgressions; but I will deliver them from all their dwelling places in which they have sinned, and will cleanse them. And they will by My people, and I will be their God. And My servant David will be king over them, and they will all have one shepherd; and they will walk in My ordinances, and keep My statutes, and observe them. And they shall live on the land that I gave to Jacob My servant, in which your fathers lived; and they will live on it, they, and their sons, and their sons' sons, forever, and David My servant shall be their prince forever. And I will make a covenant of peace with them; it will be an everlasting covenant with them. And I will place them and multiply them, and will set My sanctuary in their midst forever. My dwelling place also will be with them; and I will be their God, and they will be My people.

And the nations will know that I am the Lord who sanctifies Israel, when My sanctuary is in their midst forever' " (Ezekiel 37:21-28).

But, O Beloved, before all that or with all that, He must fulfill His word to us, the church: "In My Father's house are many dwelling places; if it were not so, I would have told you; for I go to prepare a place for you. And if I go and prepare a place for you, I will come again, and receive you to Myself; that where I am, there you may be also" (John 14:2-3).

That is where I want to be, where He is—Jehovah-shammah.

And I saw a new heaven and a new earth; for the first heaven and the first earth passed away, and there is no longer any sea. And I saw the holy city, new Jerusalem, coming down out of heaven from God, made ready as a bride adorned for her husband. And I heard a loud voice from the throne, saying, "Behold, the tabernacle of God is among men, and He shall dwell among them, and they shall be His people, and God Himself shall be among them, and He shall wipe away every tear from their eyes; and there shall no longer be any death; there shall no longer be any mourning, or crying, or pain; the first things have passed away." And he who sits on the throne said, "Behold, I am making all things new." And He said, "Write, for these words are faithful and true" (Revelation 21:1-5).

Until He comes, may everything in His temple, my body and yours, say glory to the Lord (Psalm 29:9).

Maranatha!

Remember when I asked you on the first day of our study to describe God? Well, Beloved, your last assignment in this study is to write out another description of your God. When you finish, compare it with the one you wrote on the first day. Has He taught you more about Himself? Has it blessed you?

If you want to retain what you have learned, rehearse God's names over and over again as you pray. Knowing the names of God will help you in worshiping Him properly.

Notes

1. Geoffrey Bull, *God Holds the Key* (Chicago: Moody Press, 1959).
2. Irving Jensen, *Jensen's Survey of Old Testament* (Chicago: Moody Press,1978), 360.
3. Ibid., 368.
4. The New American Standard Bible says "according to His name."

Discussion Questions for Days 39 through 42

1. What does Jehovah-shammah mean?

2. Another name for God is Qanna, Jealous. What relationship did you see between the two names, the Lord Is There and Jealous?

3. What picture did you see in your mind when you read the account of the Lord's departure from the inner court in Jerusalem? How did that affect you emotionally?

4. How would you define God's jealousy? How do you see God's jealousy in relation to yourself?

5. After God reluctantly departed from His people in the Ezekiel account, we see Him again in the person of the Lord Jesus Christ—Jehovah-shammah, the Lord Is There. He walked among them as:

> Adonai
> Jehovah-jireh
> Jehovah-raah
> Jehovah-nissi
> Jehovah-tsidkenu
> Jehovah-sabaoth
> Jehovah-rapha
> Jehovah-mekoddishkem
> Jehovah-shalom

Still they rejected Him! You have studied the names of God. You know Him as His people Israel knew Him. They rejected Him. What have you done with Him? Who is He to you? *O Beloved, may we live in the knowledge of who He is!*

A Guide for Pronouncing the Names of God

Because the English transliterations of the Hebrew words for the names of God are sometimes difficult to pronounce, the following guide is provided. Webster's *New Collegiate Dictionary* is the source for the following:

Adonai—*äd-ə-'nī*

El—*el*

El Elyon—*el 'el-yən*

Elohim—*el-ō-'hēm*

El Roi—*el rȯi*

El Shaddai—*el shəd-'dī*

Jehovah—*ji-'hō-və*

Yahweh—*'yä-(,)wā* (also Yahveh; a preferred translation of the Hebrew traditionally rendered *Jehovah*)

Jehovah-jireh—*ji-'hō-və 'ji-rə*

Jehovah-mekoddishkem—*ji-'hō-və mə-'käd-dish-'kim*

Jehovah-nissi—*ji-'hō-və 'nis-sē*

Jehovah-raah—*ji-'hō-və 'rä-äh*

Jehovah-rapha—*ji-'hō-və 'rä-fä*

Jehovah-sabaoth—*ji-'hō-və se-bä-'ōth*

Jehovah-shalom—*ji-'hō-və shä-lōm*

Jehovah-shammah—*ji-'hō-və 'shäm-mä*

Jehovah-tsidkenu—*ji-'hō-və tsid-'kä-nü*

Qanna'—*qannā'*

GOD'S PLAN

PRETRIBULATION RAPTURE
Or MID-TRIB, POST-TRIB,
Whenever . . . He is coming for His bride!
I Thessalonians 4:13-18   I Corinthians 15:51-58

**JUDGMENT SEAT
OF CHRIST**

II Corinthians 5:10   Romans 14:10

**FIRST COMING
OF CHRIST**

**ANTICHRIST
REIGNS**
Matthew 24:15   Daniel 9:26-27

CHURCH AGE   3½ years | 3½ years

John 3:16   Revelation 2-3

DANIEL'S 70TH WEEK
Revelation 6-19
Daniel 9:24-27

HADES

ABRAHAM'S BOSOM   Luke 16:19-31   **PLACE OF TORMENT**
OR PARADISE
(Vacated and taken to the
third heaven after Jesus'
death and resurrection)
II Corinthians 12:2-4

OF THE AGES

SAVED - - -
UNSAVED ———

GREAT WHITE THRONE JUDGMENT
Revelation 20:11-15

SECOND COMING OF CHRIST
(Jehovah-shammah)
Revelation 19:11-21

FIRE DESTROYS EARTH
II Peter 3:10-13

BATTLE OF ARMAGEDDON
Revelation 19:11-21

JUDGMENT OF NATIONS
Matthew 25:31-46

NEW HEAVEN NEW EARTH ETERNITY

1,000 YEAR REIGN OF CHRIST

Revelation 20:1-7

Revelation 21 and 22

Satan bound

Satan loosed

BOTTOMLESS PIT
Revelation 20:1-3

LAKE OF FIRE
Revelation 20:10, 13-15
Matthew 25:41, 46

217

For information about Kay's teaching ministry and her Precept Upon Precept inductive Bible study courses, write:

Precept Ministries of Reach Out, Inc.
P. O. Box 182218
Chattanooga, Tennessee 37422
Attention: Information Department
(615) 892-6814

Also, if you desire information on audio or video cassette teaching tapes that accompany this book on the names of God, write or call the Customer Services Department. Or, if you just want to write to Kay, she would love to hear from you.

DISCOVER GOD'S TRUTHS
FOR YOURSELF!

Every book in Kay Arthur's powerful *Lord* Bible study series is designed to help you study *inductively;* to examine God's Word in-depth and discern his truths for yourself, rather than relying on interpretations by others.

You can learn more about this life-changing study method in the revolutionary *International Inductive Study Bible;* the only Bible on the market that teaches you how to examine each book of the Bible—chapter by chapter—completely on your own.

Look for the *International Inductive Study Bible* at your local Christian bookstore.